KARATE
EMPOWERED

RICK L. BREWER

DISCLAIMER: Please note that the author and publisher of this book are NOT RESPONSIBLE in any manner whatsoever for any injury that may result from practicing the techniques and/or following the instructions given within. Since the physical activities described herein may be too strenuous in nature for some readers to engage in safely, it is essential that a physician be consulted prior to training.

First published in 2021 by AWP LLC/Empire Books.

© Copyright 2021 by AWP LLC/Empire Books. All rights reserved. No part of this publication may be reproduced or utilized in any form or by any means, electronic or mechanical, including photo- copying, recording, or by any information storage and retrieval system, without prior written permission from AWP LLC/Empire Books.

EMPIRE BOOKS
P.O. BOX 491788, LOS ANGELES, CA 90049

FIRST EDITION
Library of Congress Catalog Number: ISBN-13: 978-1-949753-32-5
21 20 19 18 17 16 15 14 13 12 11 10
Library of Congress Cataloging-in-Publication Data Brewer, Rick L.
Karate Empowered / by Rick L. Brewer -- 1st ed. p. cm.
Includes index.
ISBN 1-949753-32-5 (pbk. : alk. paper) 1. Karate. 5. Martial arts--philosophy. 3. Large type books. I. Title. GV1114.3.F715 2014 796.815'3--dc22 2006012998.

PRINTED IN THE UNITED STATES OF AMERICA.

Karate Empowered

By

Rick L. Brewer

Karate Empowered

By

Rick L. Brewer

Preface

By **Jose M. Fraguas**

TRADITIONAL KARATE IS NOT A SPORT. Someone who chooses to devote themselves to a sport such as basketball, tennis, soccer, or football, which is based on youth, strength, and speed chooses to die twice. When you can no longer do a certain sport, due to the lack of any one of those attributes, waking up in the morning without the activity and purpose that has been the center of your day for twenty-five years is spooky. Karate can and should be practiced for life. It is a "way of life."

Many of the greatest karate teachers share a commonly misunderstood teaching methodology. They know the words that could be used to pass their personal experience to their students have little or no meaning. They know that to try "self-discovery" in quantitative or empirical terms is a useless task. A great deal of knowledge and wisdom (the ability to use knowledge in a proper and correct way) comes from what is called the "oral traditions," which the art of karate-do, like every other cultural aspect, has. These oral traditions have been always reserved for a certain kind of student and have been considered "secrets." I believe these secrets are such because only a few very special students, perspicacious and with a keen sense of introspection, have the minds to attain them. As Alexandra David-Neel wrote: "It is not on the master that the secret depends but on the hearer. Truth learned from others is of no value, the only truth which is effective and of value is self-discovered...the teacher can only guide to the point of discovery." In the end, "The only secret is that there is no secret," or as Kato Tokuro, probably the greatest potter of the last century, a great art scholar, and the teacher of Spanish painter and sculptor Pablo Picasso (1881-1973) said: "The sole cause of secrets in craftsmanship is the student's inability to learn!"

This work deals with the use of karate-do principles, principles that empower us to live a better life, a fullest life with a deeper meaning.

I encourage the reader to sit alone and collect your thoughts, free from all forms of technology and distraction, and just think and reflect on the teachings gathered in this book.

I don't believe that great books are meant to be read fast. I've always thought that really good writing is timeless, and that time spent reading doesn't detract anything from your life, but rather adds to it. So, take your time. Approach the reading of this book with either the Zen "beginner's mind" or "empty cup" mentality and let the words of Rick L. Brewer Sensei help you to grow, not only as a karate-ka, but as a human being as well.

Dedication

To Donna Andres Brewer

And to

Jeremiah and Jessica

Acknowledgements

To Master Gichin Funakoshi

To my dear wife, for her unwavering love, support, and patience all these years; for putting up with my occasionally "obsessive karate quirks" all these decades. She made it all possible.

To Jim Hartman, Ted Quinn, my friend Carl L Hartter, and especially to all of my thousands of students, past and present…many who have themselves become excellent instructors and my good friends; and who are working to pass traditional authentic karate-do onto others "straight and well."

A special thank you to Jose Fraguas and Val Mijailovic for their valuable dedication and contributions to karate, and for sharing their valuable knowledge, advice, and support.

And a very especial thank you to my mother, for her lifetime of kindness and her fighting spirit! …And, to my sister, Cheryl.

About the Author

RICK BREWER is retired educator, a full-time karate instructor, regular columnist, book author, and fine artist. He regularly teaches classes and clinics in the Central Illinois Shotokan Karate Association and in the Central States Shotokan that he co-founded in the late 1980s. The Central States Shotokan Dan Certification Board awarded him 8th Dan. Brewer began formal Shotokan karate training in 1968 as a member of the Japan Karate Association (JKA), while attending Illinois State University. He has been continuously training and teaching traditional karate since.

Brewer has a Bachelors' Degree in Education from Illinois State University and a Masters' Degree in Education from the University of Illinois, Champaign-Urbana, where he completed The Leadership Development Program. He has incorporated many principles from the U of I, Leadership Development Program into developing karate students into community leaders and fine instructors. For over fifty consecutive years, he has been dedicated to developing students into black belts and outstanding karate instructors.

Brewer has been directly involved in planning, building, teaching, and assisting karate programs in YWCAs, universities, high schools, recreation centers, and commercial karate schools. Over the many years, his students have gone on to study, teach, and compete in state, national, and international venues, including the Budokan, and the Hoitsugan Dojo in Japan. His blackbelts are also serving their communities in law enforcement, military service, education, in medical professions, and the like nationwide.

Brewer was the Administrative Department Head of Career and Technical Education and a teacher at Pekin Community High School, in Illinois. Early in his teaching career, in 1975, he started the Pekin High Karate Club, wrote the curriculum and textbook, and taught one of the earliest accredited, School Board approved, Secondary Education Karate classes in the US.

In the late 1980s, he and Carl Hartter and the Central Illinois Shotokan Karate Association joined the American JKA Karate Association (AJKA) and were on the original founding Board of Directors and Shihankai of Randall G. Hassell's

American Shotokan Karate Alliance (ASKA). During his ASKA tenure, he was promoted to a 6th Dan in WUKO (World Union of Karate-do Organizations) and a 7th Dan in the ASKA.

Brewer's work reflects his admiration for pioneering martial art legends. For example: Master Gichin Funakoshi was a schoolteacher, karate pioneer, calligrapher, and poet. And the "Sword Saint" Myamoto Musashi, whose concepts permeate traditional karate-do, was greatly admired for his astonishing fighting skills. In addition to notoriety as a sword master, Musashi is famous for his written reflections in *The Book of Five Rings*, and for being a superb painter and sculptor.

As a freelance writer, Brewer has had dozens of karate related articles published in *Shotokan Karate Magazine (SKM)*, *American Profiles in Karate*, *Kick Illustrated*, *Inside Karate*, *Martial Arts Illustrated*, *Masters Magazine*, and others. Brewer was also the Technical Editor/ Reviewer of *The Complete Idiots Guide to Karate* by Randall Hassell and Edmond Otis. He did an extensive DVD interview with Sensei Randall G. Hassell for the premier issue of *Masters Magazine*. He was featured in the Shotokan Masters DVD series, published by Randall Hassell Sensei and Tamashi Press.

Brewer also paints fine art oils and does sculptures. His subjects are usually related to karate, Rocky Mountain landscapes and Mt. Fuji in Japan, wildlife such as Bald Eagles in flight, Samurai, and First Nation, American Indians.

He has written his regular *"Karate Insight"* column in *Masters Magazine* since 2012. He wrote the book, *Karate Insights: Lessons for Life*, published in 2018 by Empire Books.

One of Brewer's personal favorite quotes:

"Seven times down — eight times up!"

Prologue

To search for the old is to understand the new.
  The old, the new
    This is a matter of time.
      In all things man must have a clear mind.
        The way:
          Who will pass it on straight and well?

-- Poem by MASTER GICHIN FUNAKOSHI

KARATE DO makes participants EMPOWERED. Karate training gives one the mental and physical strength to overcome challenges that bring others to their knees. Karate-do indicates the karate "way" of peaceful conduct, integrity, and positive attitudes. It quickly becomes a prism that serious karate students begin to look through, to a clearer view of life in general, when one commits to its long-term study. It is a useful, active, life energy management method. It involves self-evaluation, reflection, and a desire to improve. Karate addresses basic needs of human survival at many levels. These principles are every bit of value today in our crazy world as ever. The needs of people to live in harmony with integrity, peace, mutual respect, courage and justice, are as grave as they have ever been.

The karate dojo opens up a new world to students entering the dojo. Karate skill sets are wonderfully scientific and powerful and have evolved for centuries. Whether we are young and strong or older and more experienced, the scientific applications of correctly practiced techniques are still one of the most effective means of empty-handed survival ever invented. Once learned, internalized, ingrained into mind and muscle memory, we always have them with us.

The mental skills we learn in conjunction with the physical are derived from cutting edge warrior studies from Japanese legends like Myamoto Musashi and his contemporaries, who lived by the sword for eons and who actually faced life and death quite objectively. Or like Shuri-te karate Master Matsumura "Bushi" Sokon. Matsumura served as head of security and bodyguard over fifty years for three Okinawan kings, and is responsible for names like Anko Asato, Anko Itosu, Gichin Funakoshi, and many others who became karate pioneers revered in Okinawan and Japanese karate lineages that thrive today worldwide. Our modern karate concepts and techniques were born of trial by fire and implementation, not theoretical notions. Those karate skills are a basis for positive mental and physical strengths, integrity, peace and harmony, justice, and for powerful, conscious, and sub-conscious directed karate actions. Karate Do empowers its students!

The codes of conduct in traditional karate are the guidelines on the road of our karate journey. Because of my background in Shotokan, Funakoshi and his peers are referenced often in this work. But all of the traditional martial arts stress positive character traits and productive lifestyles with peace and harmony.

It has been said that karate-do is a journey --- a path of travel. Karate empowers anyone who undertakes its challenges; making the effort to strive with tenacity, to move forward, trying to overcome life challenges. In a practical sense, it's easily as relevant in our senseless world today as a century ago.

It's not magic, it's not religion, it's the karate lifestyle. Karate is work and study with discipline to achieve, to persist "trying to perfect something that can never be perfected." We are always a work in progress.

Comprehensive Karate Training is Empowering!

Karate-do is a comprehensive lifelong endeavor. Funakoshi showcased karate as an art that can be practiced by the average person to enable them to be extraordinary. He wrote about and promoted karate-do for the mental and physical combined wealth of benefits for everyone. In his own words, he said that karate promotes health and fitness and "may be practiced by the physically weak, by men, women, children, and by elderly people." He said, "Each individual may adjust the exercise to his own capacity…the amount of exercise increases as training progresses."

Inclusive, Not Exclusive

Funakoshi clearly explained karate as inclusive, and as a physical education solution in the public schools of his time. Today, I know from experience, that concept is just as valuable and applicable as ever. In fact, relative to many laws of "inclusion" that were passed in the United States over the last fifty years in education, Funakoshi was in many ways a hundred years ahead of our time.

Reinvent Yourself to Overcome!

When I first read that Funakoshi was a weakling as a child who gradually built himself up through karate, I immediately saw a good fit for myself. I was a weakling as a child and bullied in my childhood years. Bingo! And when I read that his own highly esteemed teachers, Itosu and Azato, were both very weak in their childhood, but after karate training became different strong tenacious versions of their old selves," I was sold!

This should give cause to instructors whose major emphasis is only for the few physically fit competitors. You can get angry and stomp your feet at that statement, but the fact is, good people are being driven away from your dojo. One can have a dojo that teaches comprehensive karate to benefit all sorts of people, and still encourage those who enjoy tournaments. Many come to the dojo gain rebuild themselves to be healthier and gain self-esteem that they may never have had. For those who come in the dojo because they have been physically weak or emotionally beaten down, karate may be even more of a self-esteem survival necessity. They need to be empowered for emotional and physical survival and comprehensive karate experiences can make a huge difference in their lives. For those who are older, younger, or weaker, the gradual physical training is a rejuvenating experience; a renewal that can help them realize new potentials. Karate is designed for developing a better human being in a rich multi-faceted manner. They can raise their own bar with joy!

In self-defense, karate techniques "rely principally on striking, kicking, and thrusting techniques. These movements are quicker and can escape the untrained eye." Weaker, smaller people can take advantage of quick blocking, parrying, and counter-attacking techniques; especially when delivered at the same time, performed in one seamless motion from the result of practice. Karate is a great equalizer, and requires no weapons, so it is with you all the time. If the practitioner has a physical disability from accidents or illness, etc., the potential uses of other available strengths can be used.

Just as a small example: I've passed out rope to have students do partner drills and kumite with their hands tied. And I've had them spar with one hand tied behind their back, just to force the realization that they have many tools at their disposal. Instead of dwelling on the weakness, appreciate our available strengths. Mentally, we immediately go to what still works to overcome obstacles. Having had hip replacements and knee surgeries (just a fact of life; no more) has caused me inconveniences from time to time, using crutches, walkers, etc. So, when life inconveniences occur, we must take an inventory of our possible weapons. More than once, a friend (usually from karate) may tease me about being crippled and vulnerable to attack, as I quickly poke a crutch end into their groin, replying, "No they gave me weapons!"

Mental Strengths and Character building

"Karate for all," was Master Funakoshi's progressive point of view on the physical benefits of karate-do but this is still only part of the discussion. The essence of karate's mental character strengthening components are astounding. Funakoshi strongly advocated "fostering the traits of courage, courtesy, integrity, humility, and self-control."

This book is a comprehensive view of training from many of karate's founders. The teaching of technique in the dojo is up to the instructor, their style, and their intent. This is an anthology covering comprehensive content of karate-do that helps people steer their own destinies. The reader can peruse a chapter and put it down to reflect upon it in their quiet hours. The instructor is encouraged to use ideas to build and supplement lessons for class enrichment and support all of the good things they are trying to do. But above all, maybe it can help an average person learn and appreciate that karate is about the empowerment of all karate students.

Karate Empowering for All

This book is focused on EMPOWERING for EVERYONE. You only get energy out if you put energy in. That's how the human condition works. Karate training pays dividends, with astounding benefits are dramatic and effective as a result effort put in. Karate-do is participation in life with strengths of body and mind that you can build and carry with you wherever you are. You can be amazed!

Karate-do has always been comprehensive and practical. Self-defense, health improvement and wellness, stress management, fitness, social interaction with our fellow human beings, compassion, self-discipline, courage and self-confidence, accomplishing goals, increased self-esteem, and the like, are all elements of the personal power gained. The *Dojo Kun* (Dojo Code) outline main points that are posted in most dojos to remind us of our main karate goals. They are a compass pointing us in the right direction. Minoru Kawawada Sensei, Chief Instructor of the Hoitsugan Dojo, stressed in a recent visit that the *Dojo Jun* should posted in every dojo as a reminder to students of their priorities in karate training.

Dojo Kun (Dojo Code)

1. Jinkaku kansei ni tsutomuru koto
    --- *Seek perfection of character.*

2. Makoto no michi o mamoru koto
    --- *Be faithful and sincere.*

3. Doryoku no seishin o yashinau koto
    --- *Endeavor to always do your best.*

4. Reigi o omonzuru koto
    --- *Respect others.*

5. Keki no yu o imashimuru koto
    --- *Refrain from violent behavior.*

We are "Life-long Learners." We understand that we are always a work in progress, but we just keep hammering away to do our best to improve a little bit every day.

Through karate training, practitioners become "empowered" to successfully conduct the affairs in their own life. They can be refreshed and can re-boot! Think of yourself turning into that big lion or panther "who just quietly moves through his normal day, doing what needs to be done" in his world.

Back to the Source

In over fifty years of karate-do, I've attended countless clinics with some amazing instructors who are legends. I've valued, learned, enjoyed, and had been honored to train with some great senseis like Ozawa, Nishiyama, Kanazawa, Kawawada, Schmidt, Yabe, and Hassell, to name a few. Without exception, they made references back to Funakoshi and his contemporaries. In addition to experiencing every new instructional books and media that I could get my hands on; I often went back to Funakoshi's texts and biographical materials to feel like I was going back to the source. Granted, many things have improved or changed over the decades across the karate spectrum but checking back with the original sources has always been a confirmation; and always just plain fascinating!

Knowledge is Power!

One important thing all had in common was their karate lifestyle: karate-do. Much in karate empowers us all to be back in control, from life's challenges, physical attacks to mental assault, and life-threatening illnesses as well. "Karate Empowerment" puts us back into our own driver's seat! Knowledge is power!

The Mission of a Sensei:
A Word, a Spark, a Blaze.

The slightest well-aimed word
    May ignite a life-long passion for learning
karate-do.

Teaching is like keeping kindling
    Aglow during a mountain blizzard.

If teachers fan too briskly, they may clumsily
    Scatter the sparks to the wind.

The challenge is to inspire, to encourage,
    To nurture, and to lead.

Fan the desire to learn,
    Until it becomes a self-sustaining blaze.

By Author

CHAPTER 1

Empowered!

THE BASIC ORIGINS of karate were no-nonsense practical and powerful survival skills. Karate in the beginning meant that one lived in the martial mind set, day and night, as a necessity to stay alive, or to use these skill sets and to give your utmost, your life if necessary, to keep someone else alive. The empty-hand-way from Okinawan origins was like breathing, always there and necessary for survival. In a combative society with the inherent dangers from thugs, authorities, or other opposing warriors, quality weapons were a luxury a poor person would not be allowed to have. And if you were well armed in your duties serving a master as a Samurai, and you become disarmed, you had better have a backup plan! The pure beauty of karate-do is that wherever you are, you are well armed with your bare hands. Your warrior weapons are ALWAYS with you. Your knowledge and skillsets of empty hand combat are within. You are empowered with karate-do.

Studying the exploits of masters like Myamoto Musashi, Sokon "Bushi" Matsumura, Gichin Funakoshi and the like; events surrounding these great legends still seem to contradict the laws of science and modern rationality. To obsession, they trained their minds and bodies developing an indomitable spirit and technical abilities to unbelievable heights.

Karate-do training is not about mystical, smoke and mirrors trickery and the Olympic level acrobatics the media might project; it is available to YOU. Karate is both physical and mental. Your mind is the major generator of healthy vigor for an enthusiastic disposition, and it is the vehicle of conscious and subconsciously directed energies. This potentially powerful segment of karate training is sometimes neglected. Under the trained eye, something is clearly missing. There is a hollowness. By contrast, someone who has trained to cultivate both a strong mental spirit and high levels of technical skill is potentially a very dangerous person. And, when opponents are of equal physical strength and skill, the one who is mentally stronger will win. The differences are strikingly obvious. Funakoshi and his peers stress this.

Serious karate training, especially nowadays, involves the formation of a "karate lifestyle". With time, as you train, new paradigms of thinking are gradually formed. Be patient with yourself. The best karate training is developing and honing a wide spectrum of mental skills and attitudes, both conscious and subconscious. By its very nature, it stimulates comprehensive and positive character traits, while dramatically effective fighting techniques are learned and sharpened.

These, at first glance, may seem contradictory, as things in karate often do. For example, while Funakoshi taught that without a spirit of "peace, there is no true karate," he also taught that we must train to accumulate powerful karate skills that we would make even "wild beasts tremble!" It is peace through strength and confidence.

A topic often referred to as "karate spirit training" can seem intense, but no one ever said that karate was supposed to be easy. As with anything of true value that makes a profound difference, there are work and challenges involved. We often speak of having "fighting spirit" for self-defense, or in combat, when lives are on the line. Even in competition, the competitors with the most fighting spirit will win over the judges.

Clearly, many people who are quite good at karate, came to it as shy and soft spoken. Some may have been bullied. Some may just be looking for something meaningful in their lives. Many students must learn how to get rowdy when its required. But those students often make the best seasoned karateka! They can be very powerfully skilled and at the same time, are very even tempered. Dozens of my most accomplished black belts who have competed nationally and even in the Budokan in Japan, started out as shy teenagers. But now they are strong, highly skilled instructors with their own dojos who have taught national clinics. I like to blackmail them with old pictures and movies of their first days when they were embarrassed to yell and shout in karate class. But confidence, karate skills, and inner strengths grew with their karate training. But watching them teach classes, I proudly notice they have empathy for the students who may be struggling at first like they remember doing. Karate empowered them to be fine men and women who are leaders and wonderful human beings.

Good advanced, highly skilled students and instructors will look to maintain the humility of a "beginners mind." While grappling with improving and applying techniques we feel a spirit of harmony as we train with like-minded karate people and make new friends from around the world.

To beginners and observers and these concepts may seem puzzling, even contradictory. Can you really have an explosive high-spirited, vicious looking match, and seconds later be a cool, calm, and friendly? In karate-do, we would say, "Of course!" This may not make sense to the brand-new student, but they soon learn that contrasts are inherent in karate. It is the necessary balance. Develop the character of the karate student, while reaching high levels of technical ability. As an instructor, and directly from the great masters, it is a necessary and proper duty.

Webster's defines "spirit" as a "life-giving force," or the "animating" stimulant that directs your actions. In terms karate spirit training, "spirit" is the mindset or disposition you must have if you are suddenly attacked as a bad guy tries to do you in. Karate training is fascinating because it is so very multifaceted; you are learning to focus, magnify, and apply your mental skills, while transitioning explosively and fluidly through your technique. Karate is more than just punching and kicking it empowers you with the ability to keep your compass pointed in a positive direction as you face life's speed bumps.

Observe and model your character and your karate spirit after the life-force the tiny green plant that against all odds, grows stubbornly up through the microscopic, unforgiving crack, in rock-hard concrete. Appreciate on any mountain hiking trail a small, twisted pine tree, rooted stubbornly to a cliff of solid granite; admire its tenacity!

Karate is far more valuable than just preparing to fight. With correct and comprehensive karate training, we avoid crisis if possible; we strive to calmly and successfully cope with sometimes daunting challenges. Authentic karate training is preparing to be a better human being. New patterns of thinking and behavior emerge through directed mental training, reflection, and from countless experiences on the dojo floor. Our karate-do training is a motivating, driving force: a raging fire in the furnace.

Through the beauty of sincere and dedicated karate training, the human being is empowered and changed forever.

CHAPTER 2

Critical Karate Spirit Training!

IN CHAPTER ONE, I mention "spirit training" in discussing nonphysical but critical components that are actuators, powerful stimulants, and are important driving forces in traditional karate. Martial arts clearly build a personal arsenal of physical skills designed to create deadly force. With proper instruction and serious traditional karate training over time, you will stimulate your intellect, acquire an ability to control emotions, improve your integrity, and strengthen the very fiber of your character. You tap into and animate your own life forces at will: spirit training.

Karate is not easy. The legendary masters were adamant, stressing that being a good karate student means far more than the just being the big dog on the block. As Gichin Funakoshi said, karate is a never-ending process, and "there are no limits."

For example: There is an outwardly visible energy that is explosive and highly animated in karate technique. And there is the contrasting spirit that is calm, contemplative, and intellectual. We must move freely like big cat, from each motion and mind set using self-control. We use a wide range of karate components. Consistently in the literature of legendary weapon and the karate masters, training is to reach a mentally balanced, intelligent spirit.

As far back as Sun Tzu, non-violent mental ingenuity is clearly valued higher than haphazard violence and conflict. In fact, Sun Tzu expresses in his book, *The Art of War*, that "defeating even one hundred enemies without fighting is supreme." His principles have been studied through the ages, valued, and quoted often throughout all martial arts. His theories and observations are highly relevant and valued today by modern military. As you study his strategies for large and small-scale war and conflict, you easily see the genius at work in correctly applying forces.

In Shotokan, as most styles of karate, the proper comprehensive karate spirit and principles of conduct in the written "Dojo Kun" (the dojo codes of ethics and behavior) as far back as the 1700s (and probably further) to Sakugawa; an early diplomat and bodyguard for the Okinawa royal family. A student of Sakagura, the incredibly famous Sokon "Bushi" Matsumura, in the 1800s, was head of security and chief bodyguard to Okinawan kings and families for 50 years. Undoubtably, as a minister (head of security) of the royal family, Matsumura had to be extremely intelligent, courteous, and a master of proper etiquette while performing his royal duties; at least in his "day job." He was, at the same time, one of the most respected and feared fighters in Okinawa. Among others, he taught Yasutsune Itosu and Yasutsune Azato, who are famous in Shotokan as Funakoshi's instructors. Matsumura wrote his own precepts of proper behavior for his students and countless others who can still peruse them today. (You can still obtain a copy.)

Gichin Funakoshi was amazingly prolific in writing and teaching the "proper karate spirit" for his students and generations to come around the world. Not only did he stress daily karate technique training, but he was adamant that karateka develop a quality mind. Funakoshi stressed humility, courtesy, gentleness, self-composure, education, courage, health, well-being and much more! Violence was something to be avoided if possible. But, as a karate student, do not be overwhelmed by these challenges. Embrace them. Funakoshi's karate spirit training process was always a work in progress and meant long-term accumulated skills. Remember he said, "There are no limits." Karate can be for most all ages, men, women, and children, to train and practice to unlock their true potentials to be highly productive human beings.

Funakoshi's concept of karate training with the correct spirit, is the virtuous, gentle, modest person with a wealth of characteristics that include powerful effective technical skills.

This has been generally emulated and confirmed in widely known and in more modern times. Think of the popular early President of the United States, Teddy Roosevelt, whose rallying popular slogan was, "Speak softly and carry a big stick!" Behind his statesmanship and warm popularity, his "big stick policy" held the full might of his country's war machine. In more recent times, the same values of our centuries old karate values are prevalent in modern day. For example, General and former Secretary of State, Colin Powell, quite seriously responded to a question on his view of national defense policies. He said, "You do everything you possibly can" diplomatically and politically "to avoid trouble and avoid conflict." Then he said, if all that fails and you have no other choices, "You go in with decisive force to get the job done."

We are so very fortunate to have had an outstanding wealth of honorable karate masters who have been instructive in shaping the correct karate spirit training through strong and wise teaching, inspiring statements, and colorful reflections of their own experiences. This past century they have inspired millions of students world-wide. Many of us have been able to train under the first generation of incredible Japanese and Okinawan instructors who trained directly under Master Funakoshi and his contemporaries. They are international treasures. We owe it to this wealth of dedicated effort, knowledge, and superb instruction, to persevere in the tradition of training in the proper karate spirit they exemplified.

CHAPTER 3

Karate Do: Humility Tempered Steel!

"Sometimes black belts think they are big shots."
--- OSAMU OZAWA

TRADITIONAL KARATE AND HUMILITY are virtually inseparable. Think about it. Historically, karate training was often conducted in pretty humble, stark conditions: a small garden of the sensei, maybe a modest dojo, with poor lighting, affected by weather, bad heating (never mind AC), and maybe even in secrecy from potential opponents or authorities. What mattered most was the outcome of the training; the karateka. But, from those modest origins, has come the greatest karate instructors the world has ever seen.

Reflect, for example on Funakoshi slipping through the Okinawa jungle darkness to train at his master's house. And look now, to the dramatic results of the contributions that generations of karate masters from Okinawa and Japan, since over a century ago, have made. Millions, world-wide, now enjoy and benefit from the holistic life forces of karate as a result.

Karate techniques generate deadly forces, as Funakoshi said, that have the power to effectively kill an opponent with one technique (*ikken hissatsu*) while practitioners must simultaneously cultivate character with humility and self-control. Karate's deadly forces must be applied justly. The untrained might see conflicting values, while the well trained see intriguing contrasts blended with perfect balance. Karate skills tempered with humility, are like learning to shoot a high caliber rifle while learning proper firearm safety or driving a two hundred mile an hour race car without crashing and burning or plowing off into the spectators. There is clearly the unpredictable tactical element of surprise; when a well-mannered person is assaulted and must react swiftly with overpowering, extremely violent levels of trained, nearly automatic reactions.

If we combine humility and other positive character traits with physical karate skills, we can be a more well-balanced and better human being. Commenting on a lack of humility sometimes displayed by some advanced students, Master Osamu Ozawa once told me that regrettably, "Sometimes black belts think they are big shots." He said, "The most important thing about karate is that we all train together and sweat out on the dojo floor. We are all equal." Ozawa Sensei was a talented, well spoken, gentleman with sword scars he would show us on his arms from the early days in Japan, when karate was just being introduced and not well received by everyone. Osamu Ozawa was once a fighter in the truest sense, using karate to save himself on the streets from people trying to kill him with bladed weapons. He was also a movie director in Japan, directing the likes of Clint Eastwood (Dirty Harry) and Rita Moreno (the nun on HBO's series, OZ), who later came to the United States to flourish with traditional Shotokan "family dojos" (as he often called them) and his international Las Vegas tournament that still continues annually to this day.

There is humility factor built into traditional karate training. The usual minimal requirements in traditional karate to train daily are only desire and an area to stand on. All that is really essential is a good instructor, good students, and a place to train. Developing karate skill sets, while building positive character traits, are hallmarks of excellent karate training. Modest clubs easily turn out excellent students. Superior karate is being taught in gyms, rec-centers, college campuses, and humble dojos world-wide.

My own first karate "lessons" (attempts) were in the 1950s, on the front lawn of my neighbor, a very burly fireman; and my first sensei. No formal dojo, no floor, no uniform: just a sensei with students who were glued to his every word. Stationed in Japan several years just after WWII, he studied both karate and jiu-jitsu. He demonstrated techniques and smashed 2x4s with his bare hands: simple for him it seemed, but captivating to me! Soon, he had me doing basic blocks, punches, strikes. I was hooked! This humble beginning ignited a life-long desire for karate.

Humility comes in many forms. For example, even after teaching for decades, my office is my gym bag. I apologized and joked with Sensei James Yabe about my gym-bag-portable "office" at a large ASKA clinic in St. Louis. Having followed his competitive exploits since the 1970s, I asked him to autograph an old picture. I fumbled through my clutter in my gym bag for a pen. I was embarrassed! Surrounded by impatient students, I kept digging and apologizing.

Yabe Sensei stood, smiling and chuckling patiently, as I searched. "Don't worry! Me too!" he laughed, "I always carry all my things stuffed in my bag, from work to practice, then home again! Very confusing!" We had a good laugh about our similar "offices." I felt a little relieved, but still like a dork.

Even in our hectic world, there is something about the true spirit of karate with humility that just seems right.

CHAPTER 4

"Awareness" *is Not a Thing:*
It is EVERYTHING.

FOOD FOR THOUGHT: predators seek to catch victims by surprise and attack so unexpectedly, so violently, and so unrelentingly, that the victim has NO chance to escape or fight back.

No skills can save you if you are caught totally unaware.

Great White Sharks evolved for millions of years into a perfect predator. It's just what they do, and they are experts. Just off the coast of South Africa like many other similar areas, lay an island of seals, lounging around, eating, mating, and minding their own business (much like us.) The seals go for a swim to cool off or grab a meal. Lurking deeply below are twenty-foot great white sharks. Like a predatory freight train, jaws gaping, and teeth flared, they launch explosively, torpedoing vertically upwardly at thirty MPH! From the deep blue below, a ton of predator slams upward into the unsuspecting prey, leaping upward and airborne, violently shaking and grinding its unsuspecting meal. It's an amazing "Shark Week" favorite…unless you are a seal.

But for people, make no mistake, when laws of civility break down and predators get hungry, karate awareness training improves survivability. Today with the societal insanities of violent crime, terrorism, anarchy, bullying, and the like, awareness of everything around us is crucial. "If you see something, say something" is more than a slogan, it is a literal lifesaver. And with senseless ruthless homeland terrorism involving school, workplace, crowded events, and shopping center murders, maiming, and the like, high stakes awareness is more than a topic of discussion, it is a necessary life-skill for us all.

Awareness is a critical an attitude and skill one must learn for any arena of danger. Awareness is a mental state that must be active when all others are on hold. The awareness button must be in the "on" position as close to 24 hours a day, 7 days a week, as possible. Of course, there are varying degrees and types of awareness. Like anything that can be taught and learned, awareness can be divided into types for study purposes for more ease in understanding and discussion. But then all types of awareness are molded back together for a universally broad and infinite result; in other words, being aware of all that is around you, all the time.

With our human frailties, this is not even possible with the use of motion detectors and radar. But significance of being aware of what is going on around you as you move through your daily life, walking in the city, driving, cycling, enjoying recreation is a no-brainer. In karate classes we often talk in terms of being attacked and losing life or limb. The lack of awareness in seemingly harmless settings can kill. For example:

texting while driving or even walking down the street not paying attention to what is going on around you is just never a good idea. Training in awareness is direct self-protection training in the martial arts and all areas of our lives. If you are an instructor and your students are thinking only samurai had great dangers that they don't have to be concerned about, you can mention that when they stepped into a roadway, they didn't have to worry about getting hit by a bus! Times change but the threats are the same.

One concept is *Tsuki no Kokoro*, or "mind like the moon". As the moon's rays on a moonlit night softly glow on everything below it on earth, so should your attention be broad and flowing out around you, so you miss nothing within range of your senses. You perceive all both small and large, obvious and obscured, just as the rays of the moon blanket the earth.

Mizu no Kokoro, or "mind like water" is a mental state that allows your mind to be clear and calm like the glassy surface of a calm lake. It is effectively a mirror that calmly reflects accurately all that you might see as you gaze upon its surface.

Drawing from this analogy, if your mind is filled with thoughts of fear, lack of confidence, and anxiety, and "what ifs", then you cannot accurately perceive the threat and react correctly. Like the pond on a windy day, images are flawed and so would any conclusions that are drawn from them. If, however, even if you are confronted with danger, but in contrast your mind is calm and clear, you can more accurately perceive the threat and react correctly to deal with it.

In a perfect world, by combining *Mizu no Kokoro* and *Tsuki no Kokoro* in your daily training, the result is that you would be calm and clear-minded, able to accurately perceive everything large and small. You are far more able to quickly see a threat and correctly react to it. In a training, practice application, when you are sparring, gaze toward your opponent's throat but don't focus your eyes. Keep a soft but very wide field of vision, so that you will not miss the slightest movement that may give away their intent. Keep your mind clear and calm at the same time. Don't allow your thoughts to stop on any one thing…keep your attention flowing. Incorporate this into your dojo training and you will feel positive results almost immediately. It is quite amazing.

On many levels, karate training may be just the ticket to cope with your high stressed lifestyle, to bring it all into proper focus and keep you mentally and physically healthy. Make no mistake, karate is a warrior art, studied for centuries with lives on the line. But in fact, the net results forge the individual into a peaceful, stronger, more aware, and more capable human being.

CHAPTER 5

Apex

Seamless Karate:
"Unconsciously, freely, and properly."

According to Master MASATOSHI NAKAYAMA:

"At the highest stage, practitioners of karate should, in actual fighting, have posture in neither body nor mind… After a long period of practice, we can move unconsciously, freely, and properly."

To think is to die. Imagine yourself in the early days of karate: unarmed, you are suddenly confronted by a cold-blooded killer wielding four feet of razor-sharp katana. His every fiber is obsessed with your swift and brutal destruction.

Does it sound like something from a novel that could never apply to you? Then move to now. Imagine that you and your loved ones are innocently leaving a shopping center or theater some evening and are suddenly accosted by some modern version of scum, obsessed with assaulting, humiliating, or killing; hell-bent on heartlessly obliterating all of your hopes and dreams forever.

Faced with such an unrelenting predator, your only hope of survival is to react swiftly and intuitively, with purposeful accuracy and commitment. Reality check. Of course, you can only do your very best. You might be able to dial 911; but probably only afterward, if possible, if you are still alive and able. Such dilemmas offer a powerful basis and motivation for the incorporation of traditional karate-do into your life.

Under these extreme conditions of eminent attack, intellectual processes shut down, become less efficient, and in fact, can be a real obstacle to successful defense and survival. Nearly automatic intuitive responses are required. Your fate can be determined in milliseconds. The time spent on thought and the conscious deliberation normally associated with problem-solving processes, must be eliminated. Reactions must be swift, decisive, powerful, and correct. The mind and body must be appropriately trained to react in unity with as much speed, fluidity, and accuracy as possible.

But there is some real encouragement. Nakayama Sensei's comments above were clearly referring too much more than tournament prowess. At such a level of ability, at this "highest stage," someone who is confronted by an unpredicted attack can respond intuitively, rapidly, and correctly according to the situation. For example: You are carrying your groceries to your car with your family, minding your own business, and are suddenly attacked. You have no opportunity to square off with the opponent in your favorite stance, there are no rules, and no referee to shout, *"Yame!"* Your life or those you treasure most depend on your response. You must react immediately and appropriately without the luxury of a battle plan, from probably ill-prepared circumstances. In other words, from no predisposition of mindset or body preparedness, you must "move unconsciously, freely and properly" in accordance with the demands of the life-threatening situation that you suddenly find yourself in. You have no choice. Admittedly, much survival in today's environment may result from being lucky enough to be in the right place at the right time. But the odds can be greatly improved by the higher levels of awareness and the improved response abilities that come from an immersion in a karate lifestyle, *karate-do*.

If the likes of Nakayama and others see such unconscious, free, and proper action as an apex of fighting skill resulting from karate training, then, exactly how can we train to even approach this level? Realistically, the idea of taking the average "civilized" sedimentary person from any walk of life and changing them into an invincible, combat-ready warrior, prepared for sudden violent surprise attack, is doubtful. On the other hand, in the obvious realities of today's violent unpredictable world, it is ridiculous to be naïve or complacent. Through appropriate training, serious karate students can develop abilities that increase survivability as they train towards Master Nakayama's "highest stage."

And according to Hidetaka Nishiyama, in his book, *Karate the Art of Empty Hand Fighting*, **"The correct apprehension of the opponent's movements and the conscious adoption of the proper techniques in accordance with them ... are performed as a single momentary act."** Swift and appropriate responses performed in one breath, require measured and systematic training of both the mind and the body. The longer that we train, the greater are the skills that we can develop. Only dedicated disciplined training of both mental and physical aspects can result in high abilities of this type of unified action.

It is wrong to think that by being a karate hobbyist, tinkering around in one gym or another, will produce even close to desired results. If you wish to attain (or teach your students to attain) these increased abilities to accurately perceive and appropriately respond to attack, then training that is designed to build these skills must be systematically incorporated into your training and teaching curriculum on a regular basis.

Master Funakoshi, in his literature, is often stresses the importance of long term repetitive daily training that results in the "internalization" of technique. As a result of training with progressively challenging types and intensities of training experiences, skills can be "internalized," in order to become second nature.

Running off to the mountains, doing millions of techniques against trees and rocks to forge your body into a deadly weapon is quite the inspirational vision; the fabric that legions are made of. This is however, not going to be your reality. Most of us must work all day at one or two jobs, pay off home mortgages, car loans, medical bills, raise kids, and the like. Hmmmm... The trip up the mountains is sounding easier! But by incorporating consistent karate training into your lifestyle, acquiring some good measure of awareness and response skills is still very realistic. This can best be accomplished if you love training for training's sake, just to grow and improve a little each day. Train until it becomes a part of you.

Another example: In *Classical Budo*, Donn Draeger states that the movements of a martial arts master are "unintentional," taking place as naturally as fruit dropping from a tree. He says that a master's actions SPONTANEOUSLY produce appropriate results, because they have been learned through years of training and experience.

So how do we mere mortals get from a state of beginning clumsiness to masterful response to attack? Even with mythical perfection probably out of reach, we can all still attain some competent level of these valuable skills. By trying to reach the top of the ladder, if we fall short on some rung on the way up, we at least have a higher view than if we were still standing on the ground looking up, having never tried. Not trying guarantees failure. Success in increments is still success. How can we all benefit, grow, and improve from karate-do training toward these highest ideals, toward the APEX? That is what this book is about. Read on.

CHAPTER 6

Unstoppable Inspiration: Stan Schmidt

"All of us in karate have a vehicle to transmit beautiful energy to other people so that they can grow in life. It gives us the emotional strength to help others. We are all a team, and we need each other."

--- STAN SCHMIDT

STAN SCHMIDT SENSEI was a truly great man, a real karate legend. For starters, he was the first non-Japanese to be awarded 7th and then 8th Dan in the Japan Karate Association (JKA), awarded the title of *Shihan* (literally meaning) "a model for the rest," and was a member of the JKA World *Shihankai* (Council of Masters). His spirit and the contributions he made through his lessons to instructors worldwide, his written and film works, his universal friendships, and just the example he set as a quality human being are unstoppable and perpetual. It would be no exaggeration to say he has affected millions and that his example and his lessons will continue to live on. He once told me many years ago, that because of his travels and all the friends he had made through his lifetime of karate training, "I feel more like a citizen of the world, not of any one country, or place. But I think of myself as a citizen of the world."

Stan Schmidt introduced Shotokan karate to South Africa and was the Chief Instructor of the South Africa JKA and for the entire Africa JKA karate organizations. Schmidt was the product of decades in Japan, competing, training, and of building lasting true friendships with many of the elite Japanese karate masters in the world. Fortunately for us all, unsurpassed, was his profound ability to translate his experiences from his own misfortunes, struggles, conquests, and achievements, into valuable lessons to pass on to current and future generations of karateka.

Stan Schmidt was born in 1936 in the Cape Province of South Africa. He earned his master's degree in communications from the University of South Africa, where he wrote his thesis that would later evolve into his first book, *Spirit of The Empty*

Hand. He first trained in Japan in 1963, when he was 26 years old, just after getting married to Judy, in what he would later call their "three-month honeymoon-*cum*- karate expedition." Like the situation many foreign, *gaijin*, students would have been in, during his first classes he said that he "didn't understand a word of Japanese." Those karate experiences during that time always made for very colorful stories in clinics, at informal get-togethers, and in his written works.

Stan Schmidt started karate because, as a black belt in Judo in South Africa, and as one who had won many judo tournament championships; he was preparing for the South Africa Judo Nationals when he literally broke his leg! Convalescing at home and being VERY frustrated, his judo instructor visited him and dropped a book into his lap and said "Maybe it will teach you how not to break your leg. You're too wild in your fighting." The book, Sensei Schmidt told us during one of his U.S. tours, "had a strange word, *KARATE*." And that word at once captured his attention and set his karate life in motion. One phrase struck him like lightning, **"The karate man never stops training."** He mentioned this experience often to clearly drive that point home.

So, with his broken leg, his new book, with his *Budo* Spirit, he hobbled out into his back yard with a chair, and began punching, striking and blocking, etc.; all he could learn using his arms against some straw on an old wall. He says in his book, *Beyond Spirit of the Empty hand,* that he kept on until his knuckles actually formed callouses. When the doctor removed his leg cast, Schmidt was startled that his injured leg had atrophied terribly. So, then he adapted his workouts to learn the kicking from his karate book with added weight training to strengthen his legs. Gradually, as karate dominated his life, he went to Japan. From then on, the karate world would be enriched wherever he traveled. Stan Schmidt was truly an example of the "karate spirit" that always was a theme in his discussions and lessons: his transcending and unstoppable karate spirit.

Living in the Midwest region of the US, in Illinois, we were fortunate to meet Sensei Schmidt when he toured the USA to promote his first book, *Spirit of the Empty Hand.* Carl Hartter and I, representing our Central States Shotokan clubs, were served on the *Shihankai* of the American Shotokan Karate Alliance (ASKA) and on its Board of Directors for many years. This afforded our students many great training opportunities. We strongly supported Sensei Randall Hassell's efforts in AJKA and ASKA Clinics, Dan Tests, Black Belt Development, and Instructor Training Programs from the very formation of the ASKA. Over his many years of karate, Hassell Sensei had cultivated friendly relationships with many top Shotokan instructors around the world. Sensei Hassell was a brilliant instructor and author. He wrote over a hundred articles, nearly thirty books on karate, and he operated Focus Publications and Tamashi Press for years. Sensei Schmidt and Sensei Hassell quickly became great friends as he edited, published, and encouraged Stan Schmidt to publish his books and DVDs.

As a result, I was able to interview and enjoy a great many informal discussions with Stan Schmidt. Sensei Schmidt said that on one particular trip to the US, he had a dual purpose. "I came to the USA to support the World Shoto Cup hosted by Teruyuki Okazaki, and to renew my friendships with some of the great JKA masters residing in the U.S., such as Takayuki Mikami, Yutaka, Shojiro Koyama, Shigeru Takashina and others."

"At the same time," Schmidt said, "Sensei Randall Hassell, of the American Shotokan Karate Alliance (ASKA), made a U.S. book signing tour to promote my book, *Spirit of the Empty Hand*. In turn this gave me the great opportunity to meet many interesting people, and even to teach and train with many of them." We were so very fortunate to be on the receiving end of that. We hosted Sensei Schmidt during his tours, for our Central Illinois Shotokan dojos to put on regional clinics with him and Sensei Hassell. In addition to the classes taught, we learned much from informal discussions during meals and leisure time; it seemed he had just one jaw-dropping story after another! Students found him warm and approachable for questions, quite candid and bluntly honest. His creative ideas, observations of human character, and karate technique analysis were endless.

Stan Schmidt was an extremely energetic creative man. Once Sensei Hassell hosted a wonderful outdoor barbeque get-together at his home after a great day's training, and Sensei Schmidt was always animated, friendly, and surrounded by inquisitive students. He was visibly excited as he told us about new movie ideas he was working on and encouraged us all to be creative with our own karate expressions as well. He seemed never afraid to think out of the box. I confess to even having the 1970s movie, *Kill and Kill Again*, that Sensei Schmidt appeared in as the "Fly;" and yes, he even floated on air. Also, in the film, Masahiko Tanaka was featured teaching a huge outdoor class from the top of a towering platform. Even on an average day, Sensei Stan Schmidt was motivating, inspiring, and spreading the good qualities of his karate spirit to humanity, and always urging others to do the same.

His unique down-to-earth attitudes and social perspectives were insightful. He was a serious observer of human behavior. Before us was a karate sensei with two artificial hips, at a time before artificial joints were commonplace as they are now. Notably, his rather famous nickname in karate circles in Japan, since early in his training, had been "Mr. Back Kick." In his book, *Meeting Myself: Beyond the Spirit of the Empty Hand*, he notes how much he worked on his back kicks obsessively before ever traveling to Japan. I confess to shyly (but quite shamelessly) asking him to pose for a photo back-kicking me; that I treasure!

Schmidt Sensei would stress how his accident and subsequent surgeries were just one of those calamities that make us stronger. After being in a terrible car crash, he had to have both hips replaced one at a time. It had not been too long since his surgeries when he came on one trip. We were fascinated to see him getting around and moving so well. In fact, when Carl and I took Sensei Schmidt and Sensei Hassell out to lunch before the evening training sessions we were in for a treat. In the restaurant, he was discussing using the kata *Jion* for the class, as he talked, Sensei Schmidt suddenly hopped out of his chair alongside our table (not at all far from other diners) and he dropped into front stance to make some points. There may have been a few startled diners around us. Nowadays folks might get a little nervous seeing that. Later Schmidt used those points in *Jion* in the class.

In addition, Schmidt partnered up with Sensei Hassell, Carl, me, and of course with random student "volunteers" doing bunkai demonstrations from Jion. He seemed to be having fun! He switched to kumite drills, new hips and all, and was clearly enjoying himself. He was so very relaxed and poised and natural demonstrating sparring attacks. I have a nice picture of him punching my friend Carl in the face that I still enjoy viewing from time to time.

Reflections of experiences and spiritual growth from his hip surgery and his rehabilitation that he shared with us were extremely valuable. "I can actually do some techniques faster than before," he said. We could not appreciate then, that some years later, Carl and I, and even several of my instructor cohorts would have our own hips replaced. We repeatedly thought of Sensei Schmidt's stories then!

Sensei Schmidt told us one special story about being in the hospital recovering. He said he was moaning and complaining about the excruciating pain late one night to his nurse. He said she was sweet, and sympathetic but she challenged him. She said that she thought he was a karate man. And she that said she had heard that karate people were supposed to have a big fighting spirit or something like that. Her comments, he said, were a "wakeup call." That was when Sensei Schmidt got a flat rock that fit in the palm of his hand, that he could use as a portable makiwara. From then on, when he felt weakness or pain, he would punch the rock. Little by little, he would use it to heal his spirit. Is this another excellent example of the true karate spirit? Absolutely.

In his classical style, his lessons transcended physical karate. "I think recovering from serious injury makes you more seasoned," he said. "Nakayama Sensei told me that it makes you have a stronger spirit. But after recovery, I also understand that he meant you become a better person. And, that you see more of the good and bad in other people."

Sensei Schmidt was quite open and friendly, and very happy to visit with students informally after classes. Someone soon asked him if he had used karate in a self-defense situation. His example was not the simple punch-kick situation you might think, but the use of a strong mind.

"Someone is more likely to attack you when you are in a weakened state; not when you are strong." He warned. "After my hip surgery, I was pale, weak, and about 10 pounds lighter.

I was leaving my bank when two men came menacingly towards me." Sensei had shared in context that these were violent and unpredictable times in South Africa. There were many changes going on in society. "There was no way that in my condition, that I could have beaten them," he said. "When they got close, I pointed behind them as though someone else was there." He quickly motioned and shouted. (Startling several students in the front.) "Hey Johnny!" He shouted, and continued, chuckling a little. "Then, I quickly hobbled away!"

Stan Schmidt told one of my personal favorite stories about modified karate workouts after his hip surgeries, but while on an air liner. He was on one of his trips to teach clinics in the USA and to work with Randall Hassell on his books. On his plane from South Africa, a good 16-hour flight, he needed to stretch his muscles and joints to relieve some discomfort; so, he did kata on the plane! He said that his body really stiffened up, especially his hips and legs. He went back to the tiny plane restroom and did Tekki kata in as wide of a stance as the restroom size would allow. (Try it on your next flight.) But it gave him a valuable stretch, improved circulation, and a chance work off some steam. Then, after sharing his story in class, he had us all do Tekki katas standing in a narrow *kiba-dachi*, pretending we were in an airplane restroom, and do the katas with no leg movement whatsoever. It worked. But I must say, it took some thought on the first couple tries. I heard a few chuckles from others in the class as we all started in. It was certainly "interesting" to say the least. I highly recommend it to you.

Schmidt's first book, the *Spirit of the Empty Hand,* was popular and inspirational. It had been built around his Masters' Degree thesis. Some years later, along with encouragement from Sensei Hassell, Schmidt wrote a sequel called, *Meeting Myself, Beyond Spirit of the Empty Hand.* On another trip to the US, and after teaching at the annual ISKF Master Camp, Sensei Hassell organized another USA book tour for Schmidt with some additional teaching clinics. On his trip to our Central Illinois Shotokan karate clubs, I was thrilled to get a very relaxed, candid, and powerful interview with Sensei Schmidt on a variety of topics. Here is what he had to say:

First, I asked him about how he had come to write his books:

"In *Spirit of the Empty Hand,* I tried to condense the events of ten years in order to write a thesis for my Masters' degree. The facts pertaining to me and our members and were truth, but we had to manipulate time and the order of events for the sake of continuity. Randall Hassell, my publisher, assisted me a great deal and encouraged me to do this new book, *Meeting Myself*. The difference between this book and *Spirit of the Empty Hand* is that the things in *Meeting Myself* are experiences exactly as they happened. They came out almost as a flowing dialogue. Important to me is the spiritual side of a human being. I think its number five of Master Funakoshi's Twenty Precepts where he says that spiritual development is paramount; technical comes second. And this is what I've discovered in my own life. There were a few times I may have been walking around with a big ego and had it deflated by serious circumstances in as little as one second. Quite often when one is in such a weakened state, other strengths come to the forefront. And it's usually the spiritual strengths. This book is about that kind of thing."

"There may be a bit of humor and philosophy that comes naturally out. I believe I've experienced certain things that others can use as a platform to step further up for themselves. I'm so pleased that Mr. Hassell kept encouraging me, because I found it inspiring to write it, and by reading it, I want others to be inspired to go to further heights. That is what I want to do for others now."

I asked Sensei Schmidt what advice he could give to mature adults, while even though they may be past their youth, are still determined to train?

"Have you got all day? (as he chuckled) I can talk from experience, and experience is the greatest teacher on earth. At one time I wondered how long I could continue in karate the way I was going, at a very harsh pace, thinking it was the be all and end all. I was not realizing, in fact, that Master Funakoshi himself said karate must be hard and soft, forceful and gentle. The idea is to get more into the gentle, so that the forcefulness can come out automatically, without overstraining. Most people try to force their karate. Whether it's a golf swing or a baseball pitch, if you force it, it doesn't work. Over forcing and over tension, I believe destroy the body.

A person in his seventies won't have the same range of motion as they had in their twenties. They should work within their range of motion and gently stretch to maintain and improve it, depending on what their ailment is. Softness and sensible training have got to come more into it, with probably a half-hour of stretching before the class or within the class.

This also applies to young people who may be injured or sick. Get the channels grooved and then impact and power can be applied through those correct channels.

Any kata, for example, may be done in many ways: an air-like approach, gradually moving into a water-like approach, and occasionally into fire, which is explosive. But that tears tissue, and it's got to be allowed to repair, which takes longer in an older person. So, I'll do one or two sharp movements. If they work, I'll leave them because I've trained for a long time, and I know they are there. If I keep doing them explosively, it's not going to make me better; it's going to injure me. I'll just do what I call 'channel training' regularly."

Sensei, could you share some of your most memorable experiences or turning points?

"The number one turning point is that I took up judo. But if it weren't for music, I wouldn't have taken up judo. I was in band with a friend that I could easily push around in high school – I was twice his size. Then, a few years later he was throwing me all around at a music rehearsal. I took up judo and later broke my ankle. My instructor threw me this book that just said *KARATE* on it. I thought it was a book on vegetables!

I began doing karate from books until one of my other instructors, after watching us crash each other to pieces, said that I should go to Japan and learn to do it properly. That was the biggest thing in my life.

About that same time, I met this lovely lady, Judy. We got married, and she came to Japan with me and stuck through those first three months. We had a week of honeymoon on the way, and that was it. The honeymoon was over. For the rest of our stay in Japan, it was just her binding up my feet and treating my blisters.

Later in life, my auto accident and the replacement of my hips was an awesome challenge. After my first hip operation, I was totally flat on my back, in pain, and into the deepest depression of my life. One night, I lay there crying and prayed for death. Around midnight, a nurse came in quietly and stood next to my bed. In a soft and caring and yet challenging voice, she said, "Where is your spirit Mister Karate Man? Aren't karate champions supposed to have fighting spirit?" As she left, she touched my forehead and said, "Trust God."

Strength was rekindled in me. I took a flat river rock out of my bag and began striking it with my hand. My new painkiller would be a makiwara, and I would plan, act, heal, and be strong with the help of God.

There is a saying in my region that, "When you are at your weakest, he is at his strongest." My ego was gone. I couldn't do much. When I was most vulnerable, I felt that God's spirit entered and did it all for me. He had been there all along, but I hadn't been listening to his voice. That was important.

Sometimes the adversities that confront us are actually steppingstones causing us to become better. The biggest adversities cause the biggest changes. Don't give in to despondency, apathy, jealousy, bitterness, and hatred. They are opposite of the fruits of love, joy, peace, and forgiveness. If you make a mistake, make it right and forget the past, forget the bad experiences, and get on with the present. The important thing is the target or the goal that you've created or the destiny you are meant to fulfill.

All of us in karate have a vehicle to transmit beautiful energy to other people so that they can grow in life. It gives us the emotional strength to help others. We are all a team, and we need each other."

I always wondered what my heroes admired the most in people they respected, so I asked him: Among your peers are many great karate masters. What are the common traits they share that explain their successes?

"The most important one is that they are able to focus in on whatever they choose to do. We had a guy carrying out a psychological experiment in our dojo. After six months for those who stick, he concluded that there definitely was something different in the personality of students who stick with it longer. He noticed that the students with darker colored belts, who demonstrated more discipline seemed to be more orderly and better communicators.

Although I may be the big cheese in my country, I still go to Japan because I want to be disciplined. Discipline is what makes freedom. People who are disciplined can apply themselves to any field. A lot of people who are disciplined are successful in their businesses, or they are doing something good for society. Don't get me wrong, you do get dropouts, but those who stick with it are a special kind of breed. Karate is a great all-around developer of human character.

I can't guarantee that people are going to have great character. Even at this stage, that is one thing I am always trying to improve upon. I've done things and my wife will say, 'Hey Stan, what about the maxims? You say it every day, so why are you like that?' Later I will think she is quite right. I believe that discipline heads you toward a focused goal. It enables you to lead other people because you are willing to be led."

Sensei, do you have a favorite kata?

"*Chinte* is basically my favorite, but after having two hip replacement operations, two years apart, I've had to rehabilitate. Categorically, the three *Tekki kata* are my favorite from the rehabilitation point of view. I do at least one *Tekki* every day because they are manageable for my hips.

Chinte has been a favorite kata from fourth *dan* up. I didn't do it when I failed seventh *dan*, and I only failed on the kata part. My report on *kumite* (sparring) was very strong, but because my hips were so sore, I picked another kata out of weakness. My *kumite* was the best thing I've ever done, and then I go and do this kata that was too tense and basically not at seventh *dan* level. I think I went on with an apologetic attitude instead of going on and just taking it. So, I went back to doing my favorite kata, *Chinte*, and passed.

I find that *Nijushiho* is good for older people without the sidekicks. Just bring the knee up and do a soft *fumikomi*. Master Funakoshi and others from the 1920s did it that way so who am I to argue? If I were to present it in front of the young JKA people, without the sidekick, they wouldn't understand. But if it were someone of Master Nakayama's caliber, they would understand without a doubt.

I like *Meikyo* because of its smoothness, and *Hangetsu* whenever I go down to the beach or in unleveled grassy areas, or training in a hotel room. They compliment the *Tekki* factor. The *Tekki* are an open family and *Hangetsu* is a closed one. To round the whole thing off, I like *Chinte* and *Nijushiho* because they are so artistic and flowing with movement in different directions. I put them all together as my favorite.

I have one other kata I've developed during my hip injury, which is named *Uki*. It means 'floating log kata' and symbolizes a person who is downed and keeps getting up. He might be weak in one area but may produce strength in another. It came out of my experiences with an old ground-fighting expert named, Claude Chanu. He taught me for 20 years and I never beat him once. He said that one day I must start applying ground holds standing up. So, that's why I developed *Uki*. But *Uki* is only for me personally and not for anyone else."

Sensei, do you feel that training in Japan is any different now than when you first started out?

"The training has always been the same, but I've changed. Training in Japan has always been a challenge. Up until my hip operations, I always went to the instructor training class no matter what my age. Then came the hip operations. I couldn't go in there; there was no way. So, I go to courses with Sugiura Sensei which he holds every year. The people are very fine towards me.

I guess they see me as an old sensei or whatever, and they give me respect. But they are the same. There is no change in the instructor class. They are tough and they diligently practice basic technique daily.

The standard at the *Honbu Dojo* is outstanding and has never gone down. And a lot of those people don't enter tournaments. They don't think it's necessary at a higher stage. They've reached a stage of mastery. I know, because I've fought all of them, and the ones that aren't entering are some of the best! A lot of them are fantastic.

If they do win a tournament, the next day its forgotten, and they're right back to normal training, just as humble and just as disciplined. That's what I like about them."

Sensei, do you have any major concerns about the future of traditional karate-do?

"Some worry, but I look at it the other way around. We must plant good green grass, even where it's dry. It is up to the various masters in Shotokan karate and in certain other styles that I've written about in my book to create the green areas. The more green we plant, the more we're going to have. I wouldn't call it utopia. You are always going to have problems with a thing like tournaments because karate brings together such a vast mixture of organizations, nationalities, and cultures. But we all have the same karate spirit in common. After all, Shotokan karate is still Shotokan karate, with the accent on character development.

What we need are alliances where people from various countries can train together. I am increasingly traveling around to bring groups of people together to interact at seminars, demonstrations, *gashukus*, and the like.

I think there is fantastic hope because of the fact that karate is a good product. We are not just packaging it up correctly, we have such a lot to give. I don't want to say this as being rude, but if you have a good marketer, he can package excrement in a good package, and it will sell. We have the opposite of that. Karate is a good quality product and we don't even try to sell it. We are quite naïve when it comes to that kind of thing.

The beauty of what we have is going to be more important as technology advances and is controlling us, and as we find technology doing everything for us – making us lame, so to speak.

I put it plainly in the book, *Meeting Myself*, quoting Marshall McLuhan. The more you use the wheel, like driving a motor car, the more the foot goes lame because we are not using it. Any extension of our senses basically causes us to go numb in that sense because we are not using it. The lever is doing it for us, the pulley is doing it for us, and that drug will fix us up — instead of us just doing it for ourselves with the empty hand.

The "empty hand" is the most beautiful thing on earth, but people don't always recognize beauty. It is for us to make it recognizable by becoming shining lights throughout the world. If we are, through books, tapes, and movies that are put together well – not just the fancy stuff that you see which is utter rubbish – there is no end to how great karate can be, because it's so good already!"

Sensei Stan Schmidt is certainly remembered as a *Shihan* — "A model for the rest." His karate spirit, contributions, energetic creativity, worldwide friendships, and his genuine concerns for mankind, have set him apart as an outstanding human being. It would be no exaggeration to say he has affected millions; that his example and his lessons continue, inspirational and unstoppable.

CHAPTER 8

Your Karate Spirit – Roar!

MY FIRST EXPERIENCE in training to develop what we were told was karate "fighting spirit" was in a 1960's class with Chicago JKA instructor, Shojiro Sugiyama. Still in line at the beginning of class, we were instructed to growl loudly from very low in our diaphragm. In unison we enthusiastically ramped up our volume to an excruciating roar. An innocent passer-bye might have mistaken us for a choir of lions at feeding time. Sugiyama Sensei then simply said "This is spirit training." We discovered a new high-spirited resource to energize our karate. He also explained that the lower-belly roar was the correct source of a *"kiai,"* rather than the vocal cords and throat. He said that when he trained his competition teams, he like to start out by having them all roar together so they would build their correct and unified team fighting spirit before training.

With a closer physiological look: an interesting aspect about a *kiai* that directly applies to us in performing karate techniques, is that the exhaling process increases muscular group contractions, and increases extreme impact power with that correct breathing. It is much like Olympic power lifters, professional tennis competitors, and the breathing that any superior athletes use. My karate pride wants to say that we did it first: when the first karate master taught techniques designed to kill an armed attacker with one punch...but maybe that's just me. Whatever the physiological process, it certainly takes the combative exchange to another much higher level.

In the animal kingdom, a blood-curdling roar is designed and used effectively to shock and paralyze prey. Psychological effects in fighting or competition are similar and all we may need is to startle the opponent long enough to make them blink. I've seen the "spirit shout" used a fraction of a second before taking the initiative to get the opponent to mentally freeze for a split second, and then it is accompanied by taking the first initiative with an immediate attack. And it works well. This timing and stunning quality of a high-spirited *kiai* is one that students can experiment with in class with different training situations, until it becomes a habit. It makes for fun and interesting drills for students. And it can be a little extra surprise that might just make a critical difference in the fighting outcome. An exciting empowering property is that when you hear and feel your own power-shout coming out, you give yourself a mental stimulus, and lift your own spirit as well. There has been scientific interest in that the extreme shout and exhaling stimulates your own central nervous system at a primal level to perform at higher levels of strength and power.

This is one important method of increasing your own fighting spirit that is practical and proven. Anyone who has served in the military, for example, has been trained in many fighting spirit learning-processes. In my own boot camp, with Marine drill instructors, after an exhausting run of just five or six miles, we came to a big ravine in sand dunes. Our drill instructors commanded us to attack the ravine and the sandy hill on the opposite side, and to yell at the top of our empty, exhausted lungs. I heard some groaning from others. But I had been in karate for five years before enlisting and I attacked the hill with wild "joy." Fighting spirit training is critical, practical, grounded in reality, and an empowering process.

Disciplined spirit training results in your ability to apply all the psychological and physiological energies that you can muster. Your life may well depend on it. It is like the samurai saying, if you are afraid or uncertain, "tense your belly and attack!" If you only save a life just once, it will be worth it.

Like electricity in lightning, wind in a hurricane, or water in a tsunami; potential energy changed to kinetic energy and power, can be channeled and unleashed with extraordinary results. It's no different than the requirements to excel in any dynamic situation; with the obvious exception that life and limb depend on the outcome. High-spirited real-world applications are a hallmark of martial arts. A proper *kiai* unleashed with technique, creates a very evident explosive force to be reckoned with. The high decibel yell may scare the bad guy, but more importantly, it assists you in recruiting even more energy and muscle fiber to your technique. As mentioned above, according to the literature, your combined blood-curdling shout with explosive technique, excites your own central nervous system into the equivalent of a self-imposed adrenalin injection. Your high-spiritedness and the results of your training will be very visible. You may surprise yourself. The difference in effectiveness, with and without a karate spirit, are highly visible and dramatic.

With the additional focused energy, you can transform ordinary technique into EXTRAORDINARY technique. It is the difference between just going through the motions and exploding with energized action.

Along with spirit training - the injection of energy with loud spirit-shouts, Sensei Sugiyama taught avoiding "scarecrow technique." Using kata for example, Sugiyama explained that if you are just stepping through memorized karate techniques, going through the motions, even though you may look great in the mirror, then you are like a scarecrow. On the outside, you may look like you are doing karate, but you are still weak and empty on the inside: like a scarecrow looking like a person on the outside but hollow and only stuffed with straw on the inside. You must do the technique by generating energy and power from the inside-out, with correctly coordinated breathing, relaxation and tension, expansion and contraction; letting energy flow through you like a high-voltage conduit, transmitted through your technique. And so, if a student joins a karate class, but their intent is a slimmer waistline, some self-defense moves, a couple trophies, or a few belt tests, they may certainly have a new hobby: but they are really only playing the scarecrow.

As a real result, with serious study, effort, and determination, karate can immeasurably change your life for the best from inside-out. You experience martial art skills, positive attitudes, and an appreciation for fellow human beings, as well as other benefits that you never possible. Learn to *kiai*: learn to roar!

CHAPTER 7

Maximize Undiscovered Abilities!

Strive to perfect something that can never be perfected.

TRADITIONAL KARATE-DO is a lifetime journey of self-discovery and quality of life enhancement. It is a profound method of cultivating and multiplying human potentials, both mentally and physically. Historically, empty-handed fighters have had to use their bodies as weapons to avoid being bludgeoned, hacked, or shot to death. Unarmed, they trained to use every available avenue of force generation in techniques and tactics, to be able to stop an opponent in one single, swift action. Against an armed assailant, a scenario that exists this very day, there is no second chance. Historically, *ikken hissatsu* was the answer *to* stopping or killing the opponent(s) with one technique. It was not about trying harder: *ikken hissatsu* was life itself.

Maximizing and discovering your untapped potentials is not a fancy ideal to read about in a philosophy text. This is concrete pragmatic change in your life that you can see and feel. This is your perception and your interaction with your world; challenges, failures and successes. You will surprise yourself with progress toward surmounting obstacles, both physical and mental in your life. What we will concentrate on here are just scratching the surface of you using the scientific properties of your karate to generate physical and mental energy and power from within your own human potential. The unique realization is that when you learn to do so, you suddenly realize that there is more within you than you had previously understood. Soon you realize your creation of forces through technique and mental skills can transfer to attitudes and changes in confidence levels that you can use in other areas of your life.

Physically, karate techniques and training methods, painstakingly based on scientific principles, develop the ability to generate explosive forces with the magnitude and direction determined at the discretion of the practitioner: you. On a regular daily basis, karate causes us to use our energy and abilities to confront all sorts of adversities; to work through life's ups and downs with high-spirited determination. Karate character- building principles are a well-known source of resilience, strength, self-assurance, and leadership. While you may never, or we hope seldomly use karate combat skill sets in your life, you can use a world of positive karate building blocks in your life every day. Think of it as building a karate do power tool set to draw from.

Patience is a building block that we formally worked on since my first karate class. I know this because my instructor told us so. We would all sit down in line, sitting on our heels with knees bent, with our toes curled back in front kick position, aiming to put more weight on the ball of the foot. We were instructed to keep our backs straight and proud! (This of course put more weight and pain on our kicking body parts)

Then, our sensei would instruct an advanced student to walk down the line to each of us, and to stand "gently" up on our heels. If you were double-jointed...no problem. Sometimes if he heard any groaning, he we leave us there a little longer, and slowly walk around, calmly whistling, or in a low voice, telling a long story. After he was satisfied with our "patience exercise," he would shout, "Stand up! Hurry up!" Easier said than done.

However, just a couple years later I found myself in the U.S. Navy pilot training boot camp, ordered by my Marine drill instructor to assume the pushup position. His next command was, "Pushups! Forever!" Mentally, from my karate patience exercises, I was not deterred from trying. And for the next 35 years as a public high school teacher, the phrase, "This is only a patience exercise," came up from my subconscious frequently, nearly every day. So, you see, training in the physical and mental realm of karate at something as simple as stretching joints for a front snap kick, *maegeri*, transfer into unlimited inner strengths that we can use for life.

Perfecting something that can never be perfected... In karate there is an overpowering, almost obsessive drive, to perfect something that can <u>never</u> be perfected. The myth and awe associated with feats performed by karateka throughout history are quite understandable. Any time we witness someone who has cultivated a talent far beyond the norm, the results are often astonishing! Think of the astonishing skill of Olympic competitors. As I watch in amazement, trying to imagine myself in their places, I often visualize my trip in an ambulance. Their years of consistent motivation, training, and discipline result in skills far beyond the norm.

According to Nishiyama in *The Art of Empty Hand Fighting*, "The remarkable strength manifested by many individual Karate techniques, both offensive and defensive, is not mysterious. On the contrary, it is the inevitable result of the effective application of well-known scientific principles to the movements of the body." We have learned much about the scientific principles that govern physiology, kinesiology, and force generation. The accumulated forces generated by coordinated karate movements of the human body are designed to deliver an instantaneous, high-impact, shock wave. Ideally, it would take only one such technique to stop an attacker. This critical force generating skill quality is exceptionally multiplied in importance if there are multiple attackers.

Generally speaking, technique forces are equal to mass, multiplied by the speed of delivery. In the context of karate, this force is also proportional to the degree of muscular expansion and contraction that occurs. In real-world application, more than one technique may need to be delivered. Defensive applications will need to occur quickly, even spontaneously in an unpredictable and rapidly changing environment. Early in training, students strive to develop singular, strong techniques that work well in the air, against a stationary bag, or a *makiwara*, in order to develop strength and technical skill. Later on, they will learn to perform just as well, shifting rapidly from one technique to another, using intuitive responses to unpredictable attacks.

    Karate force is similar to the energy that radiates from the eye of a hurricane. Likewise, force in karate is generated from the trunk of the body and radiated outward through the extremities. Expanding, contracting, rotating actions in the abdomen and hips, synchronized with correct breathing, and supported by strong stances, generate great dynamic forces that are transferred outwardly through the involved limbs. This ability, not surprisingly, comes from training, training, and more training. The goal is to transfer energy, accumulated forces and momentum, from one technique to the next, in seamless motion.

    Whether you are doing one technique, or combinations, the accumulated forces generated by all of its components, will result in the empty-hand weapon that may very well mean the difference between life and death. Its effectiveness will at first be hap-hazard, on and off. But karate techniques are designed to generate great impact forces by using our body in a coordinated fashion by using our anatomy in nearly natural motions but coinciding with scientifically sound theory. From ancient times, this was trial by fire. Useless motions and techniques died off with their unsuccessful practitioners in battle. Thank goodness in recent times, scientific evaluation of body dynamics, kinesthetics, power and force creation, resulting impact shock wave energy, muscular skeletal motion, mental stimulation, and consequent reactions, and much, much more, can be analyzed through multiple methodology and scientific technologies. Even our watches can tell us how many steps we have taken during a day, how many calories are burned, and if our heart is still beating.

All of this leads us back to the dojo, translating into practicing correct and effective karate basics, kata, applications, and character building. Through hours, months, and years, this training leads to better physical and mental skills, a healthier lifestyle, and the cultivation of potentials we would otherwise not have known. That is why long-term karate training is meaningfully described as *Budo*, or karate-do. It is a lifetime journey of self-discovery. The sum total of such karate training points us in the direction of becoming a better human being on many levels.

CHAPTER 9

Creating Exceptional Forces

THERE ARE MANY exceptional force-creating components found within each technique. We must separate and dissect them for in depth study. After we understand their functions and importance, we can reassemble them and link entire techniques together with profound results. Dedicated study and training in developing these components so that they can be naturally performed in a cohesive manor, is a source of the many of the legendary fighting skills that are the hallmark of traditional karate. Individual techniques are seamlessly linked into strong flowing combinations that are limited only by the ability, knowledge, and imagination, of the karateka.

Major types of power generating movements or actions are used when performing techniques. Major karate books from the masters often started by explaining the importance of stances with foot placements, hip rotation, knee bending and placement, major and minor movements, etc., from the ground up. In the beginning we were confused by all the seemingly endless details. Over time and instruction, things made sense, and years later everything fell together. Still, these components are underestimated. Students can memorize the movements but only after lengthy study and repetition do they become imbedded.

In very general terms, the most popular methods of karate force production can be described as: horizontal body motion (forward, backward, side, etc.), body rotation-clockwise and counter-clockwise, up and down motions, pendulum actions, and body expansion-contractions, body vibrations, and controlled breathing. Usually these are not used in total isolation, but especially when teaching them, they should be separated to be more easily studied, and understood.

Even when used singularly or in small combinations, they take human potential energy and develop tremendous kinetic energy. These are very large energy generators and are easily visible methods for creating strong technique, even for beginners. These "force producers" depend on factors like muscular contraction and expansion, proper breathing, technical execution, synchronization, mental and physical focus, and the like. As training accumulates, the ability to use these naturally increases to instinctively produce very powerful results. In fact, each technique has forces that accumulate from bigger motions and body parts out to the contact points of techniques and into and through the opponent. The larger the combined muscular and skeletal expansion and contraction, the larger the forces you have to use.

"The positive effects of karate training are accumulative."

--- GICHIN FUNAKOSHI

Imagine that you are very athletically strong and fast, but as you charge in, you stand up, or lean too far forward, or backwards, trip over your own feet, and punch wildly without focus and with little or no sense of direction. Any power you developed with your speed has been greatly misguided like a missile sent to the wrong country, your potential effective technique and generated power has been dissipated by your cumulative error.

Funakoshi is said that "the positive effects of karate training are accumulative." The opposite can occur if negative errors have accumulated, and negate the positive forces generated by your strength and conditioning. When you practice bad habits, that is what you will do. Like data bases, if you put bad information in, you get bad information out! When you are training or teaching, and things become highly frustrating, look to back to your basics immediately to fix errors and solve problems. This analytical process is critical.

Karate is putting your ego into check and looking inward for the most basic sources of problems.

A simple example could be performing a back thrust kick as a brown belt. You are sure that your kicking foot angle is good, you are tensing your leg properly, and you lift your knee quickly and thrust hard. But each time you do, you either miss your training partner or you topple one direction or the other nearly falling. To solve your problem you kick harder, and wobble more or miss by a wider margin. Hmmm. All the while you are starting your entire kicking process, your supporting knee is not bent, you are not flat on your supporting foot, and your body core and back tension is not supporting you. Those things are fundamental for all kicking, let alone a back thrust kick. And, while your flashy looking kick might score a half-point in a tournament, in real world self-defense, when you might have time for one powerful stopping technique for each attacker, and your life depends on accuracy and maintaining balance to fend off multiple attackers, it just won't be effective.

Your Vital Force Engines

Force generating mechanisms that are built into our technique. First, let's look at some easily identifiable and major power generators. In a basic *dojo* instructional setting we often separate and simplify techniques so that students may more readily understand how to perform them, even though they are rarely applied in isolation. Practicing these movements in isolation builds muscle group strength and coordination. Combining them accumulates energy that is effective and devastating when funneled through technique.

Methods of Creating Power

Horizontal Motions – Forward, back, lateral or angular body movement that generates nearly straight-line momentum. This works with the general scientific principle of the MASS times SPEED equals FORCE. Momentum in this type of motion is generally in a more direct straight-line movement toward target.

It is kind of the similar motion of a bullet, or a dragster blasting down a racetrack. It's not easy for them to change direction, but do not stand in front of them either! We usually begin teaching these methods in basic stances moving forward, backward, side to side. Then, as students start to feel the lower body stability, driving motion, and propulsion, we teach them to switch up and use tools of their arsenal, like punches and kicks, transferring that energy into destructive shock waves, like an unleashed arrow with the added tip.

Rotation – Rotational power is created by sharp rotations of the trunk of the body using abdominal body core, hips, and legs in stance, turning either clockwise or counter-clockwise rotations. Often combined with rising or dropping motions during the rotation, the rotation can amplify other power generators, too.

A common easily seen example is a reverse punch (*gyaku zuki*), often used in combination with additional punching or blocking techniques – switching rotation directions.

This is much like the body rotation used in a golf swing or baseball batter. Sensei Stan Schmidt told us about taking Masahiko Tanaka golfing in South Africa long ago. He told us that Tanaka Sensei would swing his club incredibly hard, rotating powerfully just as you would expect a karate master might do. Schmidt Sensei said that Tanaka would *"kiai!"* when he swung and drew considerable attention from the other golfers.

Vertical Down or Up Motion – Power is generated by rapid lowering or rising of the body core with techniques. The importance of this type of force generation is that the power of the weight of the entire body is used, often with the help of gravity, with sharp dropping of the hips, that is useful in close in situations especially when large horizontal movements are impossible. These are effective uses of body weight for people that are much smaller than their attackers. For example, they can drop their entire body weight to escape a bear hug from behind if they react quickly. Instructors often use these in "stranger-danger" classes for children and for "fight-back" classes for rape prevention and the like. These are good power generating principles with nearly infinite uses.

As far as karate techniques becoming highly effective, think of a dropping punch or hammer fist down on collar bones. Also, elbow strikes, rising blocks, upward punches, and downward blocks can be power assisted with the combined vertical body movements. These should not be viewed as external body movements because they also consist of internal relaxation and tension, coordinated correct breathing, and as in all physical karate technique, the explosive energy comes from the expansion and contraction of the body.

It's easy to think of multiplying forces of a hammer dropping down, but with the downward swing turning into a shock wave that drives a spike on contact.

Pendulum Action -- This is the general description of a swinging motion of the hip and upper leg, for example, in the direction of the kick, transferring power to the leg and foot producing a kick. It's similar to using limbs like the pendulum of a clock, or a catapult lever to transfer energy from the center of the body, or from larger portions of limbs outward to the contact points of the technique. People usually begin thinking of the kick as just being power from a leg, but we always try to transfer energy from the center of our core outward to the opponent. In any karate class from beginning to advanced, you will hear instructors saying raise the knee and upper leg faster! This is simply practicing pendulum action.

Most easily seen in front, back, and sidekicks; Tilt (swing) the hip toward the kick but trying not to lean the upper body backward or forward. This is also good for close quarter knee kicking as well used to the legs, groin, stomach, ribs, etc., without using the rest of the foot or shin. At a reasonable kicking distance (allowing a safe distance from the opponent's hands) the pendulum actions to front, back, side, round kicks and others, add tremendous force and speed to the kicking surfaces. It can also add some distance to the kicks to catch the opponent off guard, without just stretching out too far and decreasing power. It takes practice but is surprisingly versatile and effective.

Body Vibration -- Still following the principle of the greater the muscle contractions, and greater the resulting forces, body vibration is the sudden and abrupt contraction of available muscle groups, with a sharp exhalation and focus (sudden tension), with a short, limited range of movement used sharply and suddenly. It is especially useful in close quarters where big motions are not an option.

The makiwara is a great teaching aid in close punches; try this with fist starting only inches away. You can also practice this on a bag, or a really good friend, but the makiwara allows you to feel as though all of your power goes THROUGH instead of stopping on the surface. Start relaxed in a natural stance. Stand inches away. Then, suddenly tense the body with a feeling of "vibration" (rather than a slow tightening of muscle groups) while exhaling sharply with a punch, focusing hard.

More than anything, the feeling resembles an "electric jolt." The idea is to abruptly switch the relaxed muscle groups to sudden and abrupt tightness! In our Tekki kata, many hand techniques utilize shorter motions and body vibration through a small sharp range of motion without actual stance movement. And delivered from a strong kibadachi (side straddled "horse stance") they are very powerful. The feeling here is to imagine your back is against the wall and opponents are front and side that must be dispatched.

Building Force Generation Skills

Most of these are large body movements easily understood and performed after some practice. It is important to start with the correct basic movements and gradually build. What we are addressing here are large kinetic energy and power generating methods. Once the motions are learned well, you can experiment with cross-training to strengthen the muscle groups used if the technique form is kept absolutely correct. You might use rubber bungee cords for raising the knee, or for stepping forward in stances have another student holding on to your backside with a cord or karate belt providing resistance. Be creative.

Focus (*Kime*)

It is critical that decisive attacking and many blocking techniques are accompanied by "focus" or *kime* on impact. Energy in the form of a shock wave is transferred to the target/opponent through suddenly hardened tissue, over an extremely short period time. Lack of focus causes the force not to be transferred, but the energy dissolves or is absorbed back into your own body. The technique will be ineffective, and the power will be dissipated uselessly. In fact, without proper tension, self-injury to ligaments and bones, with broken knuckles, etc. can result. The energy transfer and the resulting impact shock wave are nullified without focus and can be turned into a push. The difference is like being hit with a soft bean bag instead of being hit with a rock.

Stance without Exception

With a direct connection to the floor, karate stances provide a strong base that are the necessary foundation needed to launch effective techniques. No matter how powerful a race car is, if its wheels are just spinning a sliding, its energies are wasted. Good stances enhance capabilities for using muscle contractions to create explosive, propulsion-type driving movements. If your stance is weak, your technique is weakened. A house built on a shoddy foundation is a crumbling house.

Whether in offense or defense, stances offer decisive stability, potential driving forces, and more efficient energy transfer through delivered techniques.

Using Stance Connection

In stationary, moving, and rotating techniques, the pressure exerted through the heels and soles of the feet into the floor can transfer, stimulate, and multiply energy back out through the hips and torso outward into technique. This simply uses Isaac Newton's laws of opposite and equal energy reactions. If you sharply push against the floor, the floor pushes back with opposite and equal energy that you can use. By both "kicking off" of the back heel into the floor on the rear foot, while simultaneously pulling you forward with the front leg, inertia is overcome and forward attacking momentum to apply to punches and kicks is tremendous.

The training objective is to eventually gain a natural "feel" for performing these major kinetic energy-producing body movements. It takes months and years before they become "internalized" to the point that they can be performed fluidly and reflexively under the pressure of attack. These fundamentals are more easily understood at first when learned one at a time to introduce the power-producing principles. The energy created in your force generating methods above is greatly multiplied from a quality connection to the ground.

As you get older and joints have wear-and-tear from age, arthritis, and other factors, it's quite normal and necessary to have a higher stance. Blackbelts with decades of training are still going to be anchored and powerful even from a higher stance; their training and muscle memory are natural. Their experience is also rich with more weapons in their personal arsenal.

Using Combinations of all of your Energy Sources

The next extremely power-multiplying step is to link everything in the above pages into technique combinations. Instead of just a block or just a punch we merge them to block-counter scenarios. Instead of a single effective kick and a fast punch, we merge them into a kick-punch technique. As in all karate, these at the heights of skill are performed as one fluid motion. Appreciate where you and your students have come from! Each major motion to generate kinetic forces were learn one at a time, each stance to perform them from, each arm and leg technique to deliver that energy to the opponent, and of course all the timing and distance factors, and now we're combining them into combinations of two, three, or four techniques in one fluid motion. Karate is definitely not for everyone!

Students learn best by practicing the combinations forward and backward as well, but without an actively pursuing partner. Then, we add the valuable realism of an enthusiastic partner. Partner drills help students quickly see the use of technique. At first, they are thinking of just how to perform the technique and where to aim it. The defender as well, is at first frantically learning how to move out of range, block, and counter, etc. We start with one step, three step, slow and fast, assigned techniques or free choices of attacks and defenses. This is physical skill building, and mental confidence and courage building. As the success builds, then it's important to have attackers convey the "intent" to hit each other for realism.

The showing of the "intent to hit your partner" was an important aspect of any partner drills and sparring under the instruction of Master Osamu Ozawa. He was a direct student under Funakoshi Gichin, from a strong family of Samurai tradition in Japan, and at the time we hosted his clinics in Illinois, he was the most senior Shotokan instructor in the Western Hemisphere. When he spoke, we listened, and that was one point I never forgot.

If your partner shows the intentions to attack you for real, even though it is a very controlled drill, you learn to assume you will get hurt if you do not do your best. If you are used to your partner showing a high fighting spirit charging in, you will get accustomed to being on the receiving end and handling it. This is a wonderful way to spot weaknesses in lesser opponents on the street who may try to intimidate you. You will be as aware as you normally are when you are waiting for your training partners to come in blinding fast like a freight train. You will be prepared.

"In One Breath"

As students progress, they learn to connect techniques (and power generating components) so that combinations can be performed as one technique, "in one breath". This becomes possible as a natural feel for the expansion and contraction of technique muscle groups increases and the body movements become more natural. Usually, when first learning block-counter combinations, we learn the block and the counter-attack techniques separately. Then, we must put them together and use them in rapid sequence. At first, they may still be two disconnected techniques, but are now linked together and performed in timing like "the old one-two."

Later, at more skilled levels, the separation between techniques in combination becomes a blur; seamless. The power producing methods are combined and linked as a natural movement. The completion and impact from the first technique should become the simultaneous start of the expansion and contraction for the second technique (and likewise for even the third or fourth in a sequence).

While in the beginning there were two distinctly separate techniques, they later become one combined technique. The number of fluidly connected techniques and force producing methods put together is limited only to training and skill level, fitness, and imagination. We were always told in many black belts clinics that that our mind should be programed that the show-stopping technique is the third or fourth finishing technique with maximum *kime*; that the first couple techniques were just to make the opponent off balance and create openings and then finish him off, so to speak. But the main goal is to be able when you must, to take all the individual karate techniques, generate and apply the most kinetic energy your body can generate, singly or in combination, and do what is required fluidly without conscious thought. Climbing a never-ending ladder upward, means you never get to the absolute top, but each rung is progress.

Karate-do training is a life-long learning process. Repetition and the formation of correct habits is critical. In a life-threatening situation, the one technique you may have the opportunity to launch, may be the only opportunity for survival. The lives of your family including your children may be at stake. This was the source of need for the common unarmed folks in ancient times the launched the birth of unarmed self-defense, karate.

Just remember that no matter how good we think we are getting, how hard we smack our makiwara, how fast we burn out a series of punches, or how devastatingly we can kick, take a moment to pause. Master Funakoshi, Master Nakayama, and many others instructed. Karate is about forty percent physical and sixty percent mental. Karate Do is lifelong learning; a journey and not a destination.

Force Engines: Self Check List

If you are wondering if you are generating all the energy you potentially can to have your very best karate techniques, here is a "thumbnail" checklist of hints and actions you can work on. So, be sure to check:

1. To blast forward, backward, or laterally, try these. Use a sudden pressure with the heel at the start of the motion against the floor to "kick-start" the movement in order to

overcome inertia (provides dramatic initial forward thrust in lower body), at the same time pulling with the front leg.

2. You can reverse this process for a sharp backward motion, and the same for sharp, quick pivots to the side, or angular directions as well.

3. Could hip and torso rotations be used?

4. Are you using expanded proper --- Expansion, contraction, and breathing?

5. Are you using focus? (sudden contractions of all appropriate leg, torso and extremity muscles allowing for efficient impact force transfer to target)

6. Try this for body vibration. (great self-defense tool.) Stand in front of a makiwara, or a bag, or a friend who is tensing abs, only about a foot. Bend your elbow with your fist or palm-heel about waist high. Relax your body naturally.

Suddenly, strike with your hand, but at the same time, quickly tense your whole body.

7. Next repeat the drill standing further back with both arms down and loose, and your body relaxed. Then repeat! Doing it again and add just a little hip rotation. You will get the idea. You can be quick and effective by just being in a natural stance!

CHAPTER 10

Kihon: The Fountain of Youth

I TAUGHT AN ADVANCED CLASS recently in our dojo with a wide variety of ranks. I had eight to 10 black belts, ranging from *Godan* through *Shodan,* with an equal group of different *kyu* ranks. During line up, I always mentally scan the line for skill differences in order to formulate a mental class plan, to accommodate one and all, so that everyone gets good training. I could quickly see that this would be a little challenging to make the work out interesting and productive for every student. Class contained students with decades training all the way to the other end of the spectrum with only a couple of years training. I told them that during *Kihon, Kata, and Kumite,* the common thread is going to be "strong basics." With an enthusiastic "OSU!" from all, we proceeded.

In different stances, they performed single techniques, then combinations of blocking, punching, and kicking and so on. I varied the stances to individual skill abilities, and likewise, had them switching stances and moving around the floor; again, according to different abilities. While keeping lower ranks within familiar basics, I corrected and pestered them on details: foot placement, hip rotation, arm, hand, foot and leg positions, breathing, eye-direction, moving properly, and the like. At the same time, the high-spirited black belts hammered away, pouring their hearts into every technique as though there were no tomorrow! To them, each maneuver was an old friend to be embraced.

I like to avoid splitting groups into smaller classes if possible when they have overlapping techniques that all need work on, I like to see the enthusiasm rub off on each other too. I don't mind at all having black belts doing combinations of four techniques, while the intermediate are doing combinations of two, and even capable beginners doing single techniques; all at the same time.

In keeping with our "basics" theme, kata strengthens basics in varied positions and directions that add new skill dimensions simulating defense against attackers from different directions. And, kata is great practice developing technique that pushes students out of their comfort zones with new variations and positions. Students study their basic techniques and enhanced applications of technique variations in new directions: forward, backward, sideways, up and down. The black belts in class enjoyed the challenges of their more advanced katas with satisfaction from many years of training. They moved with powerful rhythm of strength and relaxation, horizontally, up and down, expanding and contracting body power. They were sweating profusely as their muscle groups fired fluidly under their control.

Then we after a break, we moved into *kumite:* my strong basics theme reminder in my introduction. "Without strong basics" I said, "your sparring will be weak! *Kumite* is a quick, eventually spontaneous application of techniques acquired through repetitive training. In surprise attacks, your internalized responses can save your life. This comes from repeating basics over and over, day after day, year after year, until quality, and effectiveness becomes natural; unconsciously performed."

Traditional karate techniques were developed a long time before the ability to dial 911. Criminal statistics indicate the average attack lasts roughly two to three seconds. You may only have one opportunity to respond. K*ime-waza*, decisive techniques, that you have practiced intensely and frequently, delivered explosively, and executed nearly without thinking, will be the most valuable.

There is no substitute for a strong foundation of basic training. It's like building a fine house or towering skyscraper. As pretty and tall as it may look, strong foundations underneath are critical. Don't build your karate skyscraper or house over a sinkhole! Fundamentals determine success. So, we started with stances, moving and switching, offensive and defensive techniques, and worked our way up through several hundred repetitions: *but all kihon.*

After bowing out of class, I listened to the after-class-chatter, hoping everyone felt tired, that they had a productive class, and good work out. They appeared exhausted, dripping wet and happy! If you teach, you know what I mean.

While I pondered the class experience in my mind, two of my senior black belts walked off the floor near me. With chuckles and very little commotion between them, they bent over catching their breath. After about forty years of karate training each, they both are admirable hard-core karate "lifers" as well. Ted Quinn began training with me when he was in high school. Then he joined the USAF and when not deployed in the Middle East or elsewhere, he was stationed in Japan. He trained in the JKA Hoitsugan and other dojos for over twelve years. By invitation, he competed and trained regularly on/with the Japanese Self-Defense Forces competition team, in the Budokan. Next to him, Michael Busha, who after college traveled to and lived in Japan, and trained in Ebisu at the Hoitsugan and Honbu dojos. With the likes of these two in my class, I felt challenged to deliver, and I tried to gage their reaction.

Suddenly, a pleasantly surprising outburst! Both aged over fifty (I'll not be specific) and still immersed in *karate-do* as their life, were laughing and saying "BASICS! Oh man, what a great workout! Basics are the fountain of youth, you know?" The other chimed in, "Yeah definitely! THE FOUNTAIN OF YOUTH!"

There you have it. Who was I to argue?

CHAPTER 11

Kuzushi Waza

Crushing the opponent's stability, posture; and turning their world upside down.

MANY OF THE LAST FEW CHAPTERS have been devoted to the generated forces built into many prime kinetic energy motions that launch our karate techniques. *Kuzushi waza* is using those forces with a timing, distance, or direction designed to destroy stability, balance, center of gravity, and any mental focus they may have. This is a disorientation of their body and mind to be capitalized upon, with usually a follow-up technique, finishing off the attack.

These actions are so valuable and show such complete dominance of the opponent that in competition they are usually awarded an instant full point, or *ippon*. To ensure the action was fully intended, credit for the finishing the follow-up punch or kick is not fully given unless it scores on them before or as the victim hits the ground. Sweeping or throwing someone to the floor, and then chasing them around to strike, just won't cut it; doesn't count.

We all really loved the kumite matches, just for the kumite! As a pep talk before taking teams to tournaments,

I would encourage my students to just go into a match, have a great time and fight! Win or lose, just have fighting spirit, and enjoy yourself! I always said, "Go buy the tournament t-shirt, give it the best you can, and just go in and fight! Enjoy! Trophies do not make any difference," I reminded them, "they are only plastic and maybe some brass, not at all real gold! So, go learn all you can, make new friends, fight and enjoy karate!"

I "lost" an interesting match at a "open style karate" tournament long ago in my competition days. I say interesting, because I really had a wonderful time even though I lost to the black belt division winner. So, in my match, I was unknown and from a couple states over geographically. My group just went to the tournament to feel the karate joy! The night before, my comrade Carl Hartter and I even ceremoniously ate shark steaks in the hotel restaurant just to set our mood. (Seemed like a good idea.)

This match was in a big ballroom on carpet. I loved doing sweeping with punching and saw immediately that my opponent's stance was high and narrow. Hmmmm. I felt like a cat watching a string as we moved around a bit. Sweeping both legs at once looked like a fun possibility, as I watched him hop around in his tempting narrow stance. So why not? He hopped toward me and I charged directly at him and swept both legs. Even on the carpet he dropped like a rock, falling much faster than I anticipated so I totally missed my follow-up punch and surprised myself as he dropped. But as his butt landed feet up, I do confess, it was fun.

Surprisingly, the judge stopped the match. The referees crawled around on the carpet on their knees searching for something. I asked if my opponent had lost a contact lens? I even offered to help look, as well. "No," they said, they were looking were looking for wet spots on the carpet, to see why he slipped and "fell." I was in disbelief. Fell? But I was having a really good time.

So, all stood up and the judges restarted the match. I felt his rhythm and that stance was like a magnet, so, I swept him again on his front leg, and punched under his guard into his ribs. A second time he dropped like a rock as I hit him. On his way down he did a wild back fist into midair and somehow scored. That happens. But I enjoyed seeing him fall. The judges all knew my opponent by name, (not a good sign) and asked if he was okay, as he climbed back to his feet. Then, honest to God, the judge bent over again, looking for the mythical wet spots, swishing his fingers around on the carpet below us. Twice I had swept him, and to my disbelief, once again the match was stopped because my opponent must have slipped on a wet carpet spot. Really?

Seeing the *kanji* on the wall, I thought, "well okay, this is just going to be for the pure joy of practicing a little *kuzushi!*" And I was really just having a great time.

"Hajime!" the judge shouted. We sized each other up and I decided maybe I should let him charge in first. As he did, I slid in with my hips a little lower than his and swept his front leg HARD. It flew up high and I punched with a *kiai* and *kime*! It was a joy. He landed really hard on his back a third time. Even I was in disbelief that he let me catch his timing coming in! I was outwardly stoic, polite, humble, and inwardly incredibly happy with my *kuzushi waza* that day. The judges helped him to his feet for yet another time.

Standing on our lines, the judges waved and fouled me out for unnecessary roughness or something? My opponent went on to win the black belt division that day. But felt great satisfaction in my spirit, I had great fun, and for certain, trophies made no difference. (And we never found wet spots in that carpet…just sayin.)

The general feeling of the Shotokan kata *Basai Dai*, is famously known as that of "storming a fortress." This is a very similar feeling to the principle of *kuzushi waza*: destabilizing and crushing your opponent's balance, posture, and confidence. Figuratively speaking, while storming the fortress is the spirit in *Basai Dai*, like smashing the walls down, you could maybe also think of the feeling associated with *kuzushi waza* as storming the fortress by opening the door and sneaking in swiftly "bringing the house down." The purpose here is not merely thinking of scoring a punch or kick for competition (although we do that after unbalancing our opponent.) The purpose of *kuzushi* is to disorient, confuse, and literally turn the opponent's world upside down. In doing this, you also destabilize and seriously upset their concentration and fighting spirit. They have no base to stand on and work from, and their inner ear may be doing summersaults as they attempt to reestablish equilibrium.

The Tekki kata are useful for practicing sweeping motions from a solid stance that would be useful in close quarters and your back was to the wall. In kumite or combat any time you sense weakness, inattention, hesitation, or the like, is a good time for you to attack with sweeps, throws, and the like. In self-defense, you can sense your opponent's timing, move yourself into position, and apply a sweep or throw followed by a "finishing" technique. Your purpose is not just the sweep, it is to put them in a more vulnerable or helpless position to increase the effectiveness of your follow-up technique. You don't have to totally knock them down with either, just jolt them off balance or disrupt their posture. Sweep their kneecap, especially with shoes on, and they are not likely to chase you far. Just destabilizing their balance allows an opening for and enhanced finishing off technique with *kime* (powerful, focused, and decisive.)

Especially in self-defense, the instant you are successful in getting them off balance, take the initiative and apply your power with the spirit of being a freight train. Actually, the better your timing and placement, the least amount of actual force is needed. Timing is everything. But in your mind and body, you need the spirit of commitment attacking with your body. Or as Musashi said, "attack with the feeling of crashing in with your hips." As you disrupt balance, you can instantly apply an effective punch or another technique against their off balanced openings to finish the process. If it wasn't enough to rattle your opponent's spirit by turning his world head over heels, you then totally deflate whatever may be left with a finishing blow.

Destabilizing the opponent, destroying balance, and totally rattling his cage is *kuzushi waza*. Do not allow them to recover their balance and regain momentum. Keep your attacker down with your high-spirited dominance and additional effort if required. Assume that if he gets up, he will use a knife or gun on you. This is especially important if your opponent is stronger, more skilled, or possibly unknowingly better armed than you.

Scoring points is flawed training for survival. This is why thinking of matches alone is not enough. Playing "tag" with punches, kicks, and strikes is not intensive enough for self-defense. *Kuzushi* is a critically important skill for you when you are outnumbered, have a brief opportunity against a stronger opponent, or maybe your opponent has a hidden weapon. Your must to be determined and have the courage to crush your opponent's aggression. With *kuzushi waza* you destabilize and crush the opponent's spirit, balance, you cause them disorientation. In real world application, do not let them recover or continue attacking.

Your goal is not just to knock them down. The practical reality of this is simply that on the ground, if they are conscious and alert (and now probably really ticked off at you), they are no longer helpless, but are a renewed danger to you. They can retrieve a weapon or pull you down to grapple and disable you. Your purpose in *Kuzushi* is to disorient, to crush their fighting posture, their balance and concentration, and to strike a decisive finishing technique mercilessly as they are most vulnerable: all in one powerful motion. *Kuzushi waza* in self-defense is opening up a split-second opportunity to disable them and render them neutral as a further threat or to allow for your escape.

CHAPTER 12

Passing on the Spirit of Karate-Do: Minoru Kawawada!

"Strive NOT to be a master, but to
BE a GOOD TEACHER."

ONE OF MASATOSHI NAKAYAMA'S most notable students is Minoru Kawawada. Kawawada Sensei started his karate training by taking tickets at the door of tournaments when he was 14 years old. Since then, karate has been his life. His mission. He grew to become a world-class competitor and instructor. In fact, under Nakayama's years of personal tutelage, and after Nakayama's passing, Kawawada become the Chief Instructor of his famed Hoitsugan dojo. In Master Nakayama's own home dojo, where international students for decades have come to live and train, Kawawada carries on the tradition to pass on his teacher's karate-do.

Minoru Kawawada, known as an astounding world class competitor, including one notable win as Grand Champion of the first World Shoto Cup Tournament with first place in both kata and kumite, is one of the superior Shotokan karate instructors of our day. For decades, my students and I have watched video in awe as he fought and performed kata in international competition. The pictures of him doing kata

Sochin are clearly imprinted in our minds. So, we have been so pleased to host Kawawada Sensei for our Central Illinois Shotokan Karate training camps, and to share his knowledge with many students from dozens of traditional karate organizations throughout the Midwest, United States. To have THE Chief Hoitsugan Dojo Instructor, carrying on Nakayama's tradition of teaching Karate-do, sharing his knowledge with our own humble classes is a treasure.

I created posters suitable for framing, that participants could get signed by Kawawada to display in their dojos. Karateka from ages eight to eighty were thrilled to get them signed as Sensei pleasantly visited with them. This was a priceless experience for "kids of all ages." Quite the contrast with clinics we've all attended, where the celebrity instructor is whisked out of sight "to undisclosed locations" immediately after teaching.

Kawawada Sensei clearly enjoys meeting like-minded karate students from half-way around the world. It's no wonder that he has been welcomed on so many continents on the globe.

As Chief Instructor of the Hoitsugan dojo in Ebisu, Japan, he continues the traditions of his teacher, and Hoitsugan founder, Masatoshi Nakayama. He welcomes international karateka to the Hoitsugan and enjoys travelling to other countries to share his powerful technical skills, ideas, and experiences. It's really fascinating to hear him tell from first-hand experiences, that the rest of us can only read about.

Kawawada has a powerfully sentimental attachment to his own memories with Master Nakayama and his wife. In fact, before coming to America for our clinics, he visited Mrs. Nakayama to inform her he was leaving. She and Master Nakayama were so important to him, he said he thinks of her with great fondness, much like a second mother. He had such respect for her that he would not just leave without telling her, even as he often travels extensively to pass on his spirit of karate-do.

"I am just a man."

When you meet him, Kawawada Sensei's humility, friendliness, and knowledge of karate-do are immediately obvious. Thanks to the hard work of Dan Cook, scheduling, making arrangements, and assisting Sensei from the Hoitsugan, and with help and cooperation with Jon Keeling of Silicon Valley Karate in California, our Central Illinois Shotokan Karate clubs were all able to host summer camps in the Midwest featuring Kawawada Sensei, who had not been to the US in many years. After seeing him compete for years, pictured on magazine covers, and on the cover of Nakayama's, *Best Karate* volumes, it was probably impossible to contain our hero-worship. He tried to adjust our perspectives immediately, waving his hand with an embarrassed smile saying, "I am just a man." His priorities were to teach karate and make warm friendships. His well-known axiom is, "Strive not to be a master, but to be a good teacher." But he is clearly an extraordinary example of both; this message and mission are his hallmark.

"Karate is Budo."

During his instructor classes, his explanations are motivating, clear, and insightful. He explains that "Karate is Budo." To improve our own teaching, he stressed first teaching simpler applications that work in self-defense and to follow them up by repeated practice. Simpler hardcore applications are best, variations can be used on a "case by case" basis, depending on the age, abilities, and condition of karate students and the self-defense needs. Likewise, Kawawada insists that kata technique be done strongly, as if in fighting, and warned "not to kid ourselves about our karate" being dependable and lifesaving, unless we work on it with that intention. He cautions that "if you don't train with seriousness, your karate will not work when you need it most."

During one instructor lesson, I remembered the old "Karate Excuse."

T-shirts. These shirts were decorated with every excuse used for NOT training or skipping classes. On "not having time to train," Kawawada enthusiastically, hands waving with each word, offered perspective pointing out that one Heian kata containing combinations of strong basic techniques, takes only about one minute to perform. Do the basic math. "Multiply the minutes in an hour, times hours a day," he said. Then, with a big smile, "You don't have just one minute to train a day?" he asked.

I was reminded of a quote in one of Gichin Funakoshi's books where he said that if you can master the techniques in the five Heian kata, you are very prepared for most self-defense situations.

One of our instructors, Michael Busha, who first trained in the Hoitsugan with Kawawada Sensei in the 1980s, relates a fond story of his own first "lesson" on this perspective of training-time priorities:

According to Michael, "I had just arrived in Japan for the first time, and I had established a pattern of attending class in the early morning at the Hoitsugan, and then heading to the Honbu dojo for more classes. At that time, both dojos were just a few blocks apart in Ebisu. One morning, as I was leaving the Honbu dojo, heading back toward the Hoitsugan, Nakayama Sensei approached!"

Nakayama smiled at Busha and said, "Good morning," and headed up to the Honbu dojo. Immediately after, as Michael walked on, he ran into Kawawada Sensei whose class he had trained in earlier.

"Oh. Where you go?" asked Kawawada.

"Hoitsugan Sensei" Michael replied, turning and bowing. "I'm sorry, Sensei, but tomorrow I am going to Kyoto, so I won't be able train." (Thinking, of course, that a little heads-up would be the proper courteous protocol.)

"What? You said you would train every day! Why are you quitting now?" Kawawada asked him.

"Oh, not quitting, Sensei. I will train again on Monday" ...as he began to shrink, feeling more than a little sheepish.

"Training is serious! It is not just a hobby." He was not smiling.

Kawawada didn't miss a beat as he scolded the young gaijin.

To say the least, the next day, Michael was in class training. Kyoto sight-seeing would be left for another day. That small conversation had an EMPOWERING effect on the young Michael Busha. Now, decades later, as he travels around for work or for pleasure, he trains wherever he can. I'm sure those words are ringing in his head.

A fun side note: many years ago, Busha, being new to Central Illinois, randomly dropped into my dojo one evening to check us out, as a possible credible group to train with. The very first wet, hard-training black belt he met, was Ted Quinn. By surprising coincidence, Quinn had trained in the Hoitsugan Dojo for years as a member the JKA, Japanese Defense-Force competition team in the 1980s, while serving in the USAF at the Yokota AB. Quinn had been there when Nakayama passed away and had attended his memorial workout. Both Busha and Quinn had trained during the same decade on different days in the Hoitsugan. These new-found dojo mates both speak fluent Japanese and had dedicated their lives to karate-do. And since that night, both still train together regularly. Again, it seems that Karate has made the world smaller!

When we've had Kawawada Sensei, we have been so fortunate to have opportunities for many candid relaxed moments. We asked why he started karate in the first place. Kawawada shared that when he "was in middle school he watched a TV series called *Karate Fu Un Ji* ("Karate Adventurer") about a karateka in early Meiji era in Okinawa." He was inspired by the "main character who challenged *bujutsu* masters while traveling throughout Okinawa. This character learned not only the essence of karate, but also developed as a human being." That inspiration has been a fortunate stroke of luck for thousands of karateka who have learned and benefited from his valuable training, competitive experiences, and teaching.

On a little free time, we took him out to my favorite outdoor target shooting range. We had discovered he enjoyed target shooting, had done it in other countries on occasion, and he asked if we could have him try it. He was quite good! My friend and another senior instructor, Jim Hartman, is a retired police officer who taught defensive hand to hand and firearm tactics for 30 years to the Peoria Police Department. He gave an official lesson in safety and marksmanship for our range outing. Then along with Sensei, we all enjoyed firing a wide assortment of "hardware." Hartman awarded Kawawada Sensei with an official police shooting medal for his excellent shooting performance. He really did quite well! Karate mental focus with eye-hand coordination definitely transfers to other useful skill sets.

"True karate is "violence prevention."

In a large general class teaching all ages and ranks, Kawawada declared that there is far "too much violence" world-over and emphasized that "true karate is violence prevention." In another insightful moment, he explained that in training "we must learn to feel some pain and discomfort in our training, so that we will be more reluctant to inflict pain onto others." Food for thought! He taught children's defense against much bigger adult attackers, and for adults to prevent and heal arthritis and injuries, he stressed relaxing and stretching at the end of practice.

He undoubtedly loved teaching and telling stories about training experiences. Kawawada equates karate-do to Budo: survival, health, and high-quality character. He high-lighted the many benefits of karate as our life-journey. He strongly advocated using the *Dojo Kun:* an outline of personal conduct to act in a constructive, polite manner, to be a better human being. He stressed that the *Dojo Kun* should be posted prominently in the dojo, so students would realize how important they were to their training in karate-do.

Minoru Kawawada teaches karate-do to build peace and friendships worldwide. He reflects the influences of his sensei, Masatoshi Nakayama, and teaches his very own interpretations. He is a great example of technical skill, power, and strength of character in genuine warmth. Kawawada is an international karate ambassador for the ages.

According to Jon Keeling, who trained with him many years in Japan, Kawawada Sensei continues to teach in a way that would make Nakayama Sensei proud. Kawawada was one of Nakayama Sensei's most personal students, and the one he trusted to teach classes at his personal dojo, the Hoitsugan. After Nakayama Sensei's passing in 1987, Mrs. Nakayama turned over the dojo to Kawawada Sensei as its new Chief Instructor.

During Kawawada Sensei's recent California visit, Jon Keeling hosted many seminars for his Silicon Valley Karate that were attended by students from a large variety of organizations. He was gratified to see so many people training together; all excited to further their knowledge and ability. He said that Kawawada Sensei did a fantastic job teaching to all levels; simultaneously blending tradition and innovation, with his abilities as a superb instructor. Frequently he explained his understanding of Nakayama Sensei's goals and vision.

According to Dan Cook, who trains and assists at the Hoitsugan and teaches English in Japanese universities, from his own years of observations and experiences, Kawawada Sensei can look at any individual and know exactly what to do or say to produce dramatic improvement. This is obvious on the outside on a technical level, but more importantly, it goes deeper and changes a student's outlook; their way of thinking about training. That type of instruction is truly difficult to find.

Karate is for all aspects of our life and our training must benefit us in all ages and conditions we become; is an important message from Minoru Kawawada Sensei. We must be life-long learners. And with axiom of "the beginner's mind," there is always more room to learn. Kawawada has a gift of looking at students and recognizing what they need to do or think in order to improve. As karate training to benefit our lives the way Funakoshi insisted, he teaches students to adapt their own karate to changing conditions and situations around them, and to changing physical conditions in themselves. Kawawada's priorities are clearly to teach superior karate and to make warm friendships. From the USA Midwest to California, the Hoitsugan in Japan, and in several continents around the world, Kawawada Sensei passes along the karate, through his own voice, experiences, and perceptions. Kawawada Sensei passes karate do along to students "straight and well."

CHAPTER 13

Intensive Immersion in Japanese Karate-do:

An American's Adventures in Japan

THE POWER OF COMMITMENT defies measurement and is a passionate driving force in *Budo*. Once, in the proper frame of mind, one has entered the dojo and accepted the challenges and rigors of karate-do, life can never be the same. Karate is the art and mankind is the medium. Just as a crude scrap of metal is shaped under the stern scrutiny of the artist's eye and forged into beauty by the skilled hands of the sculpture; so, can the human being be changed forever through karate-do according to the heroic standards of *budo*. Ted Quinn is an example of a young person entering a humble high school karate dojo in the U.S. and pursuing karate-do onto the floors of the many dojos in Japan, including the Yakota Air Base club taught by Isao Aoki Sensei, and the Hoitsugan Dojo (as a member of the Japanese All Defense Force JKA Competition Team) and competing with the Japanese team in the Nippon Budokan in Tokyo Japan.

There can be no retreat. There is only the uncompromising search for skills, improvement, knowledge, and ethics; for conquering fear and weakness, gaining the traditional Japanese karate wisdom, and accepting the challenges that lay ahead. This is a chapter of one man's persistence in seeking the sources of karate-do and aspiring to achieve those goals.

Ted Quinn is a very seasoned 6th Dan with over forty-five years of karate who trains and teaches regularly in my dojos. As a member of the Central States Shotokan Shihankai, he often regularly teaches classes and trains in the Central Illinois Shotokan Karate home dojos. He regularly trains and teaches in the Central States Instructor Development Program. He was recently featured in a Central States Seminar DVD, published by em3Video, where he can be found sharing knowledge and experiences gained from both the US and Japan. Quinn is retired from the US Air Force where he was a Master Sergeant and a supervisor of a unit facilitating military intelligence processing. He lived in Japan with his family twice for over a decade and was deployed from Japan to the middle East conflict several times performing his intel duties. With his Top Secret classified duties and his training with the Japanese competition teams, he often crisscrossed cultural lines with high-ranking officers in both the Japanese and US militaries. Through his training he was often referred by superiors as a "good will ambassador."

Quinn has come full circle in unique ways. He is currently a full-time Paraprofessional Educator in the Special Education Department at Pekin Community High School. This is exactly the school where he started his karate training in 1975 as a teenager. At that time, I had started a karate club the US to beginning my career as a full-time high school teacher. And there he was. He was always at practice and always doing extra when he went home every night and weekends. He could not get enough. He was obsessed. I saw that in him and thought this was too good to be true.

When we first met, Ted Quinn was a shy, scrawny, awkward teenager. I would never have suspected, as I twisted his fingers into a proper fist, that he would someday fight in the famed Budokan as the only American (*gaijin*) member of an elite Japanese Self-Defense Force military competition team.

Shortly into our new high school karate club, we presented an all-school karate "educational" demonstration in the gymnasium. Quinn was one of our star students. In performing team kata with a dozen or so students, relatively synchronized, he did something that I enjoy bringing up for a chuckle to this day. With two thousand students and teachers watching with peaked enthusiasm in the packed basketball gym. Quinn turned unexpectedly 180 degrees in the wrong direction in the middle of the kata - but he kept going without missing a beat, and somehow blended back in with the group for the kata home stretch. (I still have that super 8mm film to blackmail him with.) But as I watched sympathetically, I could never have imagined that in the near future, my young student would be receiving the 2nd place Kata trophy in the All-Japan Self-Defense Force Championships; presented to him by the Minister of Defense of Japan!

High school karate participants are in their teenage formative years and positive character messages are important to that age group's development. In those days, karate was new, and the top-level officials had to be educated about the real karate, not the action violent movies that were appearing in Hollywood. I touted our goals in karate's positive character building for youth. With teenage hormones and mis-guided temptations they needed good choice making skills. I drove these concepts home to administrators to promote traditional karate education.

Naturally, in our karate club practices I lectured about the *Dojo Kun*, Funakoshi's karate "precepts," *bushido* ethics, and character-building of all sorts. Quinn was always front and center; riveted with interest. I often quoted Masatoshi Nakayama Sensei as the karate icon that he has been in Shotokan. Ironically, my attentive young student would one day be in Japan, participating in Master Nakayama's memorial workout and ceremony after his passing; with Nakayama

Sensei's son presiding. This event was held in the Hoitsugan dojo, where Nakayama had lived, welcomed, and taught students from all over the world. (Nakayama's tradition is still carried on by Minoru Kawawada Sensei, as students from many continents still travel to the Hoitsugan to train.) Quinn's incredible personal journey led from listening to my humble lectures about Nakayama, to training in that commemorative ceremonial class in Master Nakayama's home. Small world.

When Quinn first arrived in Tokyo Japan, he studied under the close eye of Isao Aoki, a former student of Shoji Sensei in the JKA. Aoki Sensei was a former All Japan Champion. Aoki later changed to ISKF and is listed in Kanazawa's *SKI Kumite Kyohan* book. In the 1980s, Aoki Sensei was Ted Quinn's first Japanese instructor in Japan when at the Yakota Air Base karate club. Quinn enjoyed training with Aoki Sensei very much and they later became very good friends.

He said his first conversation with Sensei Aoki was of course about their Yakota classes. Quinn asked how long class would be; he figured two hours was probably normal. Aoki said, "It would be shorter tonight because he had to leave early. Only about three hours tonight, but normally four hours or so." Quinn said he thought like a lot of clinics he attended there would probably be discussions during that time. Nope. Mostly counting and repetition. Aoki taught the kata *Unsu* to Quinn because of his body type and skills. During that time, Ted came back to Illinois on leave to train and share his new experiences. I milked him for ANYTHING I could from his new training! Quinn did *Unsu* for our classes. Performing the difficult turning jump in *Unsu*, he seemed to defy gravity! It was wonderful! Of course, we were happy to work on *Unsu* and *kumite* with him frequently while he was home on leave.

Ted Quinn was living his "karate dream." One of his first experiences was also a great reality check that held many lessons. He went to what was a wonderful summer camp opportunity that he thoroughly enjoyed, with some small glitches.

"It was in Mie Prefecture near Kyoto," he recalls. "The camp was held in a little village nestled in the mountains. I was the only foreigner, *gaijin*. We stayed in a traditional inn, slept on futons, and ate all traditional Japanese food. Each morning we got up early and went jogging early, in cadence, Japanese style. In our uniforms we ran for an hour or more, surrounded by beautiful mountains and green rice paddies. Afterward, we had breakfast and then we trained all morning. And then, after lunch, more training the rest of the afternoon. Just name a technique and count...and it was hot! This was the hardest training I'd ever had in my life."

"At one point, I don't really remember, but I passed out. When I regained consciousness, I was in a hospital hooked up to and IV. We had been doing techniques for over four hours and I guess I became dehydrated. My body had cramped up like a pretzel and I fell to the ground. My Senseis had been telling me to relax more and we were all sweating a lot, but I had noticed that the other guys were all drinking a lot of sports drinks." Hmmm. "After I recovered, my Senseis again explained the importance of relaxing much more during technique; and in drinking a lot of fluids to keep hydrated.

Make no mistake, this time I understood. I had been burning up my body's resources by unnecessary tensing. I guess some lessons are learned best by experience."

Later, Aoki Sensei became seriously ill and went into the hospital for a year. Quinn helped him out by covering some of his Aoki Sensei's classes. Then, Aoki Sensei asked a friend in the Japanese Air Force, to introduce him to an instructor at the Hoitsugan named Norio Kawamoto. Things just kept getting more interesting for the young *karateka*!

Before leaving for the USAF and fulfilling dreams in Japan, Quinn had been promoted to Nidan in our Central Illinois Shotokan. While in Japan, he was understandably scrutinized and "tested" by Japanese karateka, to see if he really deserved to wear the black belt that he earned in the United States. Afterall, this was the Japan Karate Association, and their standards were notoriously high.

They tested this new *gaijin* any chance they could. At one clinic, during a relatively basic lunge-punching drill, a middle-aged looking Japanese gentleman surged quickly toward Quinn and punched him in the mouth. Instinctively, feeling his mouth guard with his fingers, he shoved back to the roof of his mouth, he reached in and pushed it: suddenly Quinn remembered he was NOT wearing a mouthguard, and he had just shoved forward and repositioned his front row of teeth! With some ice and a bloody towel, he enjoyed a long train ride back to the Yakota Air Base with fellow passengers staring at him in wonder. (The base dentist said that immediately pushing his teeth back in place — thinking he was replacing his mouthguard — saved his own teeth.) But all things in consideration, seeing his determination, skill level, and competence, he soon earned the respect of his Japanese counterparts and made lifelong friends.

Once, "just for the experience with no real expectations" Quinn said, he entered the annual All Japan Self-Defense Force Championships. Competing were hundreds of experienced black belts from all branches of the Japanese military. It turned out to be more than just an experience, when to his surprise, he placed 8th in kata. He was admittedly "shocked" to get past the first rounds of eliminations in this caliber of an event that he only entered as a "training experience." He quickly made many new Japanese friends including Yoshitoma San, a four-time Japan Self-Defense Force Kumite Champion. Quinn was invited to train with the team at headquarters branch of the JKA for the Japanese military, JASDF, that trained regularly in the Hoitsugan Dojo.

One day, instructors borrowed his Central Illinois Shotokan 2nd Dan rank certificate for the senior instructors to closely examine. He was not sure why but immediately complied and did not ask. Apparently, he passed inspection, and was soon tested by at least one of Masahiko Tanaka's senior instructors and was awarded *Sandan* in the Japan Karate Association.

Stationed at the Yakota AB for the first of his two 6 years in Japan, he taught the base karate club as its Chief Instructor. He learned to read, write, and speak fluent Japanese; that he incorporates into our classes today. While stationed at the Yakota, Quinn traveled to Ebisu regularly training in the Hoitsugan dojo.

Quinn was living his dream. Quinn met the 4-time kumite champion of the JKA, All Japanese Defense Force Championships, and who was the JASDF military Team Captain. The two quickly bonded and Yoshitoma Sensei invited Quinn to train regularly with the Japanese Defense Force team. Rather ironic, I think that my *gaijin* student and good friend was in the United States Air Force, and became a member of the Japanese military, Self-Defense Force Karate Team. Of course, as a result, he competed in the Budokan, in the JKA All-Japan Championships.

He imposed a rigorous schedule on himself. He was full-time USAF and teaching classes on base three nights a week and taking the train to Ebisu each week to train in the Hoitsugan. "In the Hoitsugan, workouts were four hours minimum. These were straight workouts with no lectures," Quinn explained. "Most of the people I worked out with were

3rd Dans and above. Many had been champions at one time or another from Tokyo, Hokkaido, etc. We worked on basics, sparring drills, free sparring, lots of Heian and black belt kata. I was told that right above us in the building is where Nakayama and his family lived. And that Mr. Osaka and Mr. Kawawada had been photographed for the *Best Karate* series on the very floor that we were training on!" (In 2018, the author and his students hosted Sensei Kawawada in Central Illinois for a summer camp. Quinn and the rest of us spent much quality time with Kawawada Sensei. We all enjoyed his instruction and his stories thoroughly. And Kawawada Sensei happily autographed our *Best Karate* books!)

Soon after he began training with the Japanese military group in Ebisu, he received a surprise. Just a week before an up-coming JKA All Japan Championships, he was again invited to be the only non-Japanese member of the Hoitsugan, military Defense Force team. What an honor for the young Air Force NCO. From his hometown club, to becoming a member of an elite military Japan Self-Defense Force team in the All-Japan Championships! (And humbly but shamelessly, as his first instructor, I could not have been prouder)

While the five-man JASDF karate team fell short of the finals that year, two team members beat all of their opponents. One was Yoshitoma-San, the team captain, and the other was Ted Quinn.

I had asked Quinn if he recalled how well some of the older Japanese instructors did in the dojo training with some of the "younger studs." He grinned at one fond memory and said, "One time I was watching our senior Hoitsugan team instructor, Norio Kawamoto Sensei, sparring with one of the younger Sandans. The young guy ran in at him at him attacking with a barrage of techniques. Kawamoto shifted behind him quickly and grabbed his collar and pulled his uniform top over his head!"

Another fond memory of Ted Quinn's Japanese adventure is a JKA, All Japan Youth Championships that he assisted with. He had the opportunity to work the event, at a time when the Japan Karate Association was still more cohesive before its division turmoil. Quinn worked helping very famous instructtors like Asai, Abe, Kawawada, Oishi, Tanaka, and many others, all working together. "This was one of the biggest events I had ever seen." He said, "I was the only gaijin helping, and my job of all things, was to keep all the kids in line. You should have seen the look on their faces when I gave orders to them in their native tongue! When I shouted instructions at them in Japanese, their mouths dropped open and they had pure shock in their eyes."

"When Nakayama passed away," Quinn said, "I was invited to attend his memorial workout. During the ceremonies, we formally paid our respects to his memory with an inspiring dedication observance, and then we were honored with a vigorous workout. Presiding over the momentous occasion was Master Nakayama's son."

On the lighter side, Quinn accidentally entered a "full contact" tournament and was disqualified for "contact." Go figure. According to Quinn, "It was an International Friendship Tournament. I owed some Goju-ryu friends of mine a favor and they asked me to join them entering. We soon found to our surprise that it was a full-contact tournament (and no gloves)."

"The matches were really sloppy. We were pretty disgusted. And even though it was full contact, no punching to the face was allowed. The opponent I fought won the tournament. He came charging in wildly with body punches and kicks. He came in swinging, seemingly out of control, and I just unconsciously stepped back and nailed him in the face. He had a strong attack, but his face was wide open. It was just automatic after years of training. It didn't seem like as much skill was required if you don't have to worry about someone punching your face."

When Ted came home on a thirty day leave in the midst of his competing, I could not wait to ask him an important question. I asked how our training had prepared him for his transition to the intensity of his experiences in Japan. He said, "Students here should know that the Shotokan training that they can get in even small clubs in the US is quality traditional karate training. Good training is good training. I had absolutely no trouble making the transition from our dojo to the dojos in Japan. In fact, I showed my Yakota assistant, Tomio Sakamoto, and some of my Japanese friends a video of one of our Dan-grading exams. They were impressed and quite surprised to hear the commands in Japanese! My main point is that even in small clubs like our YWCA's, rec-centers, and other traditional dojos in the US, we have quality karate training."

After returning to Japan, he experienced a couple highlights of his lifetime. Yet again, for the JKA All Japan Championships, he was invited to fight on the Ebisu, five-man military kumite team and they finished in fourth place. He soon competed in the All-Japan Self-Defense Force Championships in a field of several hundred black belts. After many rounds of competition, he chose kata Gojushiho Sho, and won 2nd place! He said, "Competition was tough! There were several hundred black belts from all the military branches in Japan!" Having narrowly missed first place standing, he was shocked again. This soft-spoken karateka stepped forward to receive his award. **His trophy was presented to him by the Minister of Defense of Japan!**

During his years until 2007 living in Japan, he was stationed at the Misawa Air Base. He spent these years still teaching and training, and occasionally competing in the JKA club with several other Japanese instructors. This time it was unique as he was the only *gaijin* teaching and he taught large mixed Japanese classes with many youths, under the watchful eye of their parents. Quinn felt honored that Japanese parents were so supportive of him teaching their children. And, of course, the students were again quite shocked to hear the American teaching, explaining, and ordering them around in Japanese verbiage. The Japanese parents were quite supportive and would advise him to literally hit their sons who did not try hard enough in his classes. The American instructor was quite surprised at the extent of parental support.

But in addition to being tough, the American had his "tenderness of a warrior" side. "When I was teaching one night at the Misawa dojo, located on the second floor of the Misawa City Budokan, classes were 3 hours long, four times a week. I had taken the young beginners and running them through some basics when I felt a tug on my sleeve. I turned around and one of the kids was pointing at a very small boy crying. I went over and asked (in Japanese) what was wrong. Between sobs he said he was scared. This was his first night and I realized that he was scared because he heard this adult, not to mention a foreigner, yelling (that was me counting). I told him that was my karate voice, and he had a karate voice, too. After that he was fine."

Often things that came from this foreigner, pleasantly surprised his Japanese friends, as well. "One thing that seemed to make an impression even on the parents, was something I said while we were in *seiza* just after reciting *dojo kun*. It was customary for the instructor to say something after the recitation. Our students had just done well at a tournament and after the instructor to my left was done speaking, he looked to me to see if I had anything to say. I had just learned a new *kotowaza* (proverb) — "*Katte, kabuto no o wo shimeyo!*" which means, "When you've won, tighten the chinstrap on your helmet!" Basically, it meant for them that just because they had won a tournament, do not sit around and enjoy it, but get ready for the next battle! When I said this, there was an audible gasp from the students. I didn't think it was that big of a deal. Several of the parents often brought it up at parties for a time afterwards, wanting me to repeat it!"

"One-time Iida sensei taught a *gasshuku* at their dojo. "It was for the Taisho University students. Misawa Air Base was in the middle of a full-blown training exercise, but I managed to get over there for a couple of hours a couple of nights. I was introduced to Iida sensei, and I told him he was famous in America for *Jitte* in the *Best Karate* series. He laughed and said he had forgotten all about that. During the training, Kawamura Sensei was standing by and occasionally telling my sparring partner that it was ok not to hold back with me. I found Iida sensei to be very friendly. He signed my *Best Karate* book!"

"A lot of times I would watch or listen for how the instructors taught, always looking for a better way to instruct in Japanese. I had heard the instructors say on occasion, "*Koshi wo otose!*" (Lower your hips!). So, I tried it out, using the same stern pronunciation as I had heard. The class I was teaching, all in front stance, all as a unit, went lower. It was so cool. Like trying out Open Sesame!"

Ted Quinn was able to renew old friendships that held treasured memories. "Because I had been helping so much at the dojo, the head instructor Kawamura Sensei paid for me to go to Tokyo and compete on the Misawa team at the annual JKA championships at the Nippon Budokan."

"At some point I was watching some of the matches from up in the stadium, when I got this thought in my head that Kawamoto sensei, my original instructor at Hoitsugan in my first years in Japan, might be there. I hadn't seen him for 10 years and I remembered that I had heard that he had shaved his head, and I should be looking for a bald person. Sure enough! I found him watching a match. He had no hair just like I thought. I walked up to him and just stood there quietly. He looked at me for a few seconds, and then you could see it dawned on him who I was. He grabbed my hand and led me to another section where a bunch of the people I used to train with at the Hoitsugan were sitting. After a short visit, Kawamoto sensei said he had to go. I hung around, talking about old times with my friends and remarked about him shaving his head. Sadly, my friends told me that Kawamoto sensei had cancer. He passed not long after that, when I was deployed again in the Middle East."

Rewards for Quinn are not measured by brass trophies or plaques for the wall, but by the kinships born from thousands of hours on the dojo floor in the Hoitsugan and competing with his friend's half a world away. He fought side by side with Japanese champions on the Japanese military teams.

Quinn enjoyed occasional military social events (sometimes awkward) between officers and including NCOs. He was thrilled when several of the Japanese officers, who attending regularly, were also senior karate instructors. They would officially be there to socialize with American officers, but when they would see Master Sergeant Quinn across the room, they would immediately greet him like an old friend! Some American officer eyebrows would raise. His Air Force senior officers gave him an "Ambassador of Friendship" award before he left Japan.

Through the art of karate-do, Quinn's character has been hammered and forged by sweat, bruises, and the challenges on the dojo floor. Karate-do done with the intent and dedicated training outlined by the great masters can transcend the barriers of culture, nationalism, race, religion, and politics, because it fulfills the universal needs of human beings.

CHAPTER 14

Seizing the Initiative

THROUGHOUT THE WRITTEN HISTORY we find that of many of the ancient masters, Musashi in his *Book of Five Rings*, as one example, based much of their training concepts on "*SEN*," taking combat initiative. Many of those were transmitted easily into karate, where there are countless strategies and tactics based on taking the initiative one way or another. In empty hand combat, especially against weapons, mastering the initiative is life or death. Imagine peasants in Okinawa, for example, trying to defend their families against sword-swinging killers and they were required to be weaponless. Their inventive genius was all important and legendary.

Another favorite literary resource is Masatoshi Nakayama's, *Best Karate* series. A couple of the more frequently discussed variations of sen in karate training are "*Sen no Sen*" and "*Go no Sen*."

Generally speaking, *Sen No Sen*, is considered to be taking the initiative first, attacking a weakness or overwhelming the opponent by a "shock and awe"-type of high-spirited attack. *Go no Sen is* taking the initiative later, but in an equally powerful, overwhelming manner. In studying *Go no Sen*, you quickly realize it is not just waiting.

When watching two skilled fighters, it may not be clear who is really actually planning what. Since competition and combat are quick and fluid, fighters quickly test each other.

However, for introduction to students, we usually simplify *Sen no Sen* as "attacking" first and say that *Go no Sen* takes the form of counter-attacking. Of course, it's not that simple, but easier to understand for initiates.

CONTROL of the "initiative" is essential. In a tournament it can determine points; in combat, life or death. In the latter, there is no second place. "Taking the initiative first" can take different forms. Most obvious is after sensing openings: being aware of weaknesses, breathing patterns, or the slightest telegraphing twitch of a muscle, and then attacking explosively with no hesitation. If you don't see an obvious opening at first, you can *kiai*, feint, and cause one. Overwhelm with your spirit and intuitive tactics!

"Taking the initiative later," *Go no Sen*, is perceiving the situation as it unfolds and pouncing on opportunities during the opponent's attack. This is **not** merely waiting. It can be actively or passively "causing" the opponent to attack in exactly the manner that you want or baiting and setting a trap. You will acquire your own favorite "taking the initiative" methods. These skills are required in virtually all martial arts, are extremely useful in competitions, and without a doubt critical in self-defense, but also in business, politics, and other arenas. Most important is that we can understand and seize initiative when necessary...own the initiative!

When teaching beginners, you can assign who attacks (takes initiative) first (*sen no sen*). This puts their partner in the position of learning to turn things around to take the initiative later (*go no sen*). This is simply one-time sparring at first. You can tell them what techniques to use, or you can just assign who goes first. They'll learn fast. It becomes very enjoyable in a karate class partner drill setting.

With advanced students, instructors can ramp it up. They train to, as Hidetaka Nishiyama has said, "unconsciously attack" and take initiatives without having to think. The more you train, the easier it becomes. Time to think is a luxury that you may not have. S*en no sen* becomes more natural with accumulated training. You can quickly see opportunities or lure your partner into a mistake by either passive or active means, and then explode into a decisive first attack. You own the initiative first!

Go-no-sen, taking the initiative later, may appear as merely waiting to see what happens in order to counter, but be careful. Your opponent may actually decoy you into doing exactly what he wants you to do first: and then pounce! Just food for thought: If the "waiting" partner does even the tiniest, subtle thing, to entice the other into initiating their "desired" first attack, then who is really doing *sen no sen*? Hmmm…

In any case, Nakayama said there are three general kinds of openings to watch for: mental openings, openings in posture, and openings in movement. Ideally, our goal is to internalize technique to take immediate advantage of any of these: correctly "seizing the initiative." These are strategies and tactics we can spend endless enjoyable years working with, rarely perfecting, but every once in a while, you can experience an "Ah! HA!" moment! Welcome to karate! Whether capitalizing on taking the initiative earlier, or later, it is critical to overcome in conflict…own the initiative!

CHAPTER 15

The Extraordinary James Yabe

THE FIRST TIME I noticed Sensei James Yabe was in a photo standing on stage with the USA team in the 1970s, in the All-American Karate Federation publication called *Samurai*. He was a member of U.S. National Team at the 1970 WUKO Championships in Japan and the 1972 WUKO Championship in Paris. This dates me for sure, with any of you that read *Samurai* as well as it came off the presses. If you have never seen James Yabe in action, you were always in for quite a treat. The last I saw of him he was humbly apologizing for his bad stance due to some really serious leg injuries. To have that stance at all, we all thought enviously, would have been a gift!

In fact, if you have ever watched him train, you *knew* you were in for a treat. In any case, you'd better watch closely. Inevitably, he will tell his class what he is about to demonstrate. Then he will do it so amazingly fast, that he leaves most scratching their heads. Watching him, reminds me of the old observation of watching a master swordsman, "Does the man move the sword, or is the sword moving the man?" And should you ever have the chance, don't be afraid to ask him to show you again. He is one of the most amiable, humble, and yet skilled instructors you'll see put on a uniform. This is from an article I wrote after we attended a weekend of Yabe's clinics that covered karate in great depth. At that time, he looked young and sharp, even in his 60s; Sensei Yabe's technique was jaw-dropping! He is a most highly regarded instructor.

In classic Shotokan style, from his stance, very low and strong, he still delivered fast, sharp technique with impeccable focus, that could be rivaled by none. As far back as 1961 he was the first All-America Karate Tournament Champion in both Kumite and Kata. And he continued to firmly dominate the American Shotokan scene by winning again and again in 1962, 1963, 1966, and in 1967.

Since he began training in 1958, Yabe had trained with some of the most renowned karate masters in the United States and in Japan, and he was one of the most senior students of

Hidetaka Nishiyama in the U.S. Yabe was the Chief Instructor of American Shotokan Karate California. In 2004, Yabe joined the American Shotokan Karate Alliance (ASKA) and was the ASKA Technical Director. From experience, I must say, taking some of my own dan exams in the ASKA Headquarters with Sensei Yabe sitting at the judges' desk in front of me, was an intimidating honor.

Randall G Hassell said that, "Sensei Yabe is a living legend in JKA-style karate. The unique experience and wisdom he brings to our Alliance is virtually without peer. Personally, I often look to him for guidance and example, and I am delighted that he is able to provide his wisdom to the entire ASKA membership along with our affiliates and friends."

James Yabe's teaching was brilliant! His teaching style delivered superb technique that you are excited to copy, and his smile, humility, and openness clearly invite you to be inquisitive. In addition to radiating his obvious love for karate, his approach to teaching actually reflects his engineering career background in California as well. He presents karate theory and dynamic concepts in very analytical and understandable layers that he builds on throughout his class. Starting from a strong foundation (most obviously low stances), he artfully drew relationships from one concept to the next, leading you from simple to complex skills. All the while, his sense of humor relaxed you and his energized demeanor and enthusiasm motivated you, as he progressively increased the degree of difficulty and kept you challenged physically and mentally. We had great fun as all the while he gradually raised the bar.

One prime example: at an ASKA clinic in St. Louis, Yabe was teaching the kata Kanku Sho in a very enthusiastic and crowded gymnasium. In his unique teaching style, he flawlessly performed and coached us on each technique's technical elements and applications. Then teaching *Kanku Sho*, he came to the turning leap and drop to the floor. Before demonstrating, he turned with a big grin toward the class, saying, "When I was younger, I used to jump and turn way up in the air before coming down. Now, I don't think I can go so high." Then, waiving his arm in an upward spiraling fashion high into the air, he said, "But if you want to jump up there, you go ahead." We chuckled at the varying possibilities when it was our turn. Immediately following his little joke, he spun, leapt, and landed; nailing a technique that would put most 20-year-old competitors to shame. Attempting to follow suit, our class energetically followed his example with, well, "very mixed results!"

Consistent with his style, he continued putting us through the paces with the fundamentals and skill-building, progressing from simple to complex, challenging and inspiring all the way. Our clinics progressed with *kihon*, *kata*, and *kumite*. He stressed powerful stances with a relaxed upper body. We pressed ahead, as he stressed the importance of charging in with the hips and legs as a power-generating engine to delivering punches in a *sen-no-sen* fashion with the upper body relaxed. This was classical Shotokan; low, powerful charging stances, with fast, sharp punching with instantaneous, strong linear attack. Students were surprised to acquire new abilities in covering ground, attacking, and catching their partners, before they were able to react or escape. The room was filled with brown and black belts.

All were charging at each other with their enthusiasm unleashed; sweating, yelling, punching, kicking. This was high-spirited karate training, punctuated in the end with a few new bruises, tired legs, and happy karateka, sweating and grinning from ear to ear.

Most of the day's participants were experienced black belts with decades of training. They were men and women from a wide variety of backgrounds, ages and professions, with a common passion for learning karate who were in for quite a pleasant surprise. They were seasoned veterans and instructors in their own right who are not easily impressed, and they had trained with many other notable senseis in the USA and abroad, including Japan. I asked for their reactions to training with James Yabe. This is what some of them said:

Jim Stahly, 5th Dan and Central Illinois Shotokan Karate Association instructor in Bloomington, Illinois, gets right to the point, "Watching him do technique — or a combination of techniques — is inspirational. I don't think I've ever seen a stance quite like his. His combinations blend obvious power and explosiveness with speed and flow ... you watch him do a series of techniques, and what's going through your head is: "I want technique like THAT! Sensei Yabe's way of showing how basic techniques and kata are applicable to kumite and actual self-defense, really spells out why the points we work on so hard are so incredibly important. He shows how and why the smaller points of technique are anything but small."

Yabe's pace and energy increased so that even by the last part of the clinic, kumite training, we were going at close to full force with strong basics still remaining a primary focus. I heard advanced black belts speaking gratefully for the many individual suggestions they received. The sessions were helpful in terms of what we learned from Sensei Yabe for both our own training, and for what we could use to help improve our own teaching.

Yabe conveyed the feel for the kata, *Kanku Sho*, by offering guidance in timing and the emphasizing the relationship of *kime* to relaxing. The high level of spirit in Yabe's clinic brought students to a renewed commitment to the art of karate. He was always exemplary in his low, controlled stances (despite of any discomfort he may have been feeling from his injuries), his speed, and his driving force. We received the best of instruction, extraordinary technique, wise guidance, demanding directives, and had great fun!"

One seasoned black belt, Carlos Yu, a neurosurgeon by profession, commented,

"One of the things that impressed me most about Mr. Yabe was his demeanor. His technique of course is superb, he is confident, but modest, and able to bring out the best in a student. I enjoyed the way he presented the kata. And despite the fact that we worked on advanced kata and kumite, what was most evident to me was the importance of the basics. One has to practice stance and body movement continuously to be able to do more advanced body movements. I think everybody could see how great the technique of Sensei Yabe is."

Sandan John Garls, who has been training for decades and is a retired computer expert for a major US industrial firm has yet another perspective. More life experience causes a certain mature appreciation of the true long-term value of karate training. For many like him, it is the simplicity of a clean, well-performed, power-generating technique that holds the essence of strong karate. And that is exactly what he found in Yabe's teaching. When asked what was one of the most valuable things he had learned from the day's instruction, Garls said simply, "My instructor had been telling me for years that I needed to get into a lower stance. And suddenly I see this man who is, very impressive and still several years older than me, getting pretty low in stance, and moving very fast. Then, he came up to me and told me personally that I needed to get lower too, because he said he sees black belts all the time not getting low enough. When I tried it like he showed me, I noticed an immediate improvement in my driving force. If my legs ever get done being sore, I'm going work on it more back home."

Any instructor can be a mere conduit for the transfer of information. There are even more than a few instructors who can confuse you or put you to sleep. And, quite frankly, there are still a few others who are so arrogant that they give you the feeling, that they will gladly take your check to the bank, but that you are really too dumb to ever learn their particular level of skill. But most important of all, there are still many who are very good at creating an excitement and a fascination that lingers, long after the clinic is done. They inspire and create a thirst for more learning.

Josh Dalcher is a computer technician from Denver Colorado and Nidan with years of experience. On Yabe's unique and contrasting style, he commented that, "It was very easy to tell that Sensei Yabe truly enjoys his art. His personality exudes it... you only need to hear him talk for a few minutes to know that he lives his life to experience karate and to share what he has discovered with others. He was very quick with positive and constructive feedback that made it very easy to be motivated to train for hours on end. Even exploring advanced topics, Sensei Yabe made each element very easy to understand. In between sessions, Sensei was quick to enter conversations with his students and get to know them."

"Sensei Yabe's technique was astonishing... it seemed in very stark contrast to his easy-going personality. To see the lightning speed and raw power of even one reverse punch you know that you're dealing with a true master."

"Yabe sensei's technique was amazing!" said Matt Dukes. "Sure, his stances were lower than I'd ever seen anybody do, and his kicks seemed effortless. But what really amazed me is that when I first met him, I thought he was about 20 years younger than he actually is. Yabe shows you what a human being can do if he keeps at it."

There is a tremendous honesty in James Yabe that is captivating. The testimonials outlined here from the experienced black belts from all walks of life, portray easily observable qualities that can be nothing else but genuine. His technique was mesmerizing, his teaching abilities exemplary, and he spontaneously conveyed his genuine passion and love for karate-do in every turn. It is obvious that he enjoys karate just for the sake of doing it.

When you observe James Yabe in action, the lines of comprehension begin to blur, as in the samurai-level skill I mentioned in the first paragraph. You will wonder… "Is the man moving, doing karate, or is the karate moving the man?"

CHAPTER 16

Teaching Methods: Empowering Toward the Higher Stages

A Curriculum: Students Learning Intuitive Responses to Attack

THIS CHAPTER is a condensed curriculum, lessons, and learning paths that instructors can use to teach students the higher skill sets in karate, that can be empower them with correct reflexive counter-attack skills. It is a project summary of years of study, experimentation, and disciplined training. It starts with new people that begin training and leads to outcomes of highly expert skills being learned: to levels of internalized techniques and applications launched from "no posture of mind and body," as discussed by legendary masters.

This is a sample map of understanding paths of how students may reach the levels of skill described by karate legends as being nearly automatic, conscious and unconscious actions. It is only an outline to be considered a tool for thought stimulation and use.

Introduction

In the case of surprise attack, having to think can waste valuable time and be disastrous. Intellectual processes become inefficient, or nonexistent, and can be a serious obstacle to survival. Fate can be determined in milliseconds. Mental and physical reactions must be swift and accurate. When push comes to shove, correct, nearly reflexive responses to situations are required.

Masatoshi Nakayama said, "at the highest stage of karate, practitioners should in actual fighting, after a long period of practice with hard and painstaking training, move unconsciously, freely, and properly."

Nakayama said one has to react to defend themselves from "no particular posture of body or mind." In other words, we should be able to react instinctively in self-defense from no particular prepared state of mind and body. You may have to defend your life or your loved ones, without the opportunity of being prepared ahead of time and without the time to logically figure out what to do.

Realistically, taking the average, sedentary, "civilized person, "who is just working day to day to get by, and changing them into a skilled warrior, always prepared for a sudden violent attack, is probably unrealistic. But, with training towards Nakayama's ideas as long-term goals, as he specified, one can improve the odds of successful survival. Absolutely, there are no guarantees, but with training we can develop tools to improve survivability.

Systematic training can increase awareness, assessments of dangers, and powerful "internalized" karate techniques to use.

According to Hidetaka Nishiyama, we must learn to have 'the correct apprehension of the opponent's movements and the conscious adoption of the proper techniques in accordance with them."

Echoing Nakayama's wisdom on the importance and urgency about the swift mental awareness of the danger and use of physical responses using karate techniques; Nishiyama stressed that, "both parts are performed as a single momentary act." Both masters leave no doubt of the importance of thorough long-term training, learning to be aware of attacking opponents and being able to respond correctly and very swiftly.

Systematic Training Products

If we step back and approach karate training from a systematic teaching standpoint, starting with an untrained beginner, we begin a journey leading them along the karate lifestyle that, with their own motivation, can result in the higher intuitive stages of attack responses. We begin with an orientation.

People come from all walks of life and all ages into our dojos. I have 60-year-old active black belts now who I started training with me when they were sixteen. Most trained continuously from an inner drive. And though life threw them some curves, you may take the person out of karate, but they proved that you cannot take karate out of the person, if it is their path. Some had intermittent experiences and combat deployments, others, careers in law enforcement, some in education as teachers, and others in business and industry. Life experiences influence karate training, and karate influences life experiences. What we are looking at here are the possibilities that good karate training brings to the table.

Pretraining

Neophytes start with very little or no karate technical skills, and little or nothing in the way *Budo* mental training; they may be equipped with nothing more than their natural reactions to danger like indecision, fear, panic, or even react as an angry wild raging bull. Survival may be left to chance.

For example: Think in terms of Drivers Education and the progressive skill levels of driving. With no safe and correct driving skills, a driver may react unpredictably if danger suddenly unfolds on the road ahead. A young or easily distracted driver may even panic, throw their hands up and scream...and crash and burn. Then there is the infamous road range. What could go wrong? An experienced driver will have more mental and physical skills and better reaction times to at least narrowly escape accidents. But at the highest stages of driving, are Nascar and Indy 500 drivers who stretch envelopes and can perform without thinking in high speed incredibly dangerous, life and death, tight spots!

Prior to training we act instinctively, whatever that means, depending on the individuals. Lacking any training our reactions are unpredictable. We may freeze up and panic, flail fists wildly, and the like. We may react, or we may not. Young and older people alike may not even recognize there is danger until it is too late.

This is before awareness education has begun. For children (and adults,) it can be before they've experienced "stranger danger" lessons. Children are victims in many environments, we can teach them valuable awareness skills to avoid many dangers, but not all. As instructors, you should consider yourself a "mandatory reporter" any time you suspect a minor is being abused. We need to do what we can to build bullying barrier skills in both children and adults. EDUCATION is POWER. For many adults who watch the news, they see the problems in others but may not realize they need to be aware in their own world. And of course, depending on their life experience, this is before they may have learned any physical avoidance behaviors, or defensive physical skills to deal with aggression.

The more "civilized" and pampered society becomes, the more helpless average individuals become in the face of raw uncivilized aggression.

Introduction to Karate Fundamentals

This is the beginning of karate training. At this stage, mental ideas are introduced that will later become mental skills, attitudes, perceptions, and disciplines. This is the orientation level when karate technique fundamentals are introduced that later become internalized powerful actions if students continue training. A new world is introduced that differentiates the immersion into karate within the dojo, from the outside world. In Western societies, this may be a small "culture shock." But that's just fine and can be refreshing. The dojo, whether it's only a small rec-room or a well-built commercial facility, is understood to be a place for serious karate study. Students are taught to leave their normal busy day at the door, as they bow and say "Osu!" as they enter. Courtesy and respect are taught between students of different levels and toward instructors as is necessary in the dojo learning environment for the best learning of karate-do to take place.

Self-discipline is introduced as students are guided out of their normal comfort zones. New unusually high levels of awareness are introduced about surroundings and daily environments, such as positional awareness in restaurants, walking down the street, shopping, walking in parking lots, and even entering, or in one's own home.

The new technical karate skills come with new repetitive muscular demands that often bring sore muscles and new physical discomfort. Some people welcome this, others move on. Those that stay are rewarded by becoming physically stronger and pleased with there new knowledge of using their body as an empty-handed weapon. The introductory stage is a period of self-exploration, success and failures, coping with new and unique demands, developing new mental skills, ultimately overcoming and breaking previous personal barriers. This is a time of major curiosity, discovery, increased workloads, and new positive mindsets that can all lead to long term rewards.

New Empowered Skill Sets

In these introductory stages the body has to adapt to being used in different ways. Hand and foot defensive and offensive techniques, stances, other body movements, new breathing techniques are introduced and practiced with enthusiastic importance. Students may be wondering, "Why, or how do I do this?" The hundred repetitions that come along with technique lessons build new "muscle memory." Partner training and using these new karate skills makes it easier to understand them and apply them. As they "sink in," techniques become gradually more familiar and easier to perform. Students will carry these introductions throughout all of their advanced stages, so it is critical that any training and habits learned are good ones. The mental and physical skills learned now, transfer all the way up through the higher levels of training. That's why we teach the correct performance of basics from the first day, and we never stop.

Internalization Begins with Strong Basics

After periods of diligent repetitive practice. Very basic skills start to become "internalized" to the point that if an instructor says "punch!" students can perform an immediate punch without thinking about it. It may not be perfect, but mind-muscle connections are forming. They don't have to think about how to perform the punch, they can just do it. Since this is just the beginning of internalization, the number of techniques with the same ability is small. More complex technical internalization requires much more training and experience. Fortunately, as Gichin Funakoshi said, training just ten minutes a day is important because the "effects of karate training are cumulative."

As practice takes the shape of *Kihon*, *kata*, and simple partner *kumite* drills, a "core" of karate skills, that have been practiced the most, begin to be internalized to the point they can be used with reasonable success upon demand.

Practiced together, mental and physical skills start to become more unified and useful. The ability to use them under real stress, however, is still weak. Reactions are not quite to the stage where they can be used unconsciously but they are helpful and improving, and far better than nothing. The core of really dependable techniques may just be some basic blocking, punching, and a couple types of kicks. The "good news" is that according to crime statistics, most self-defense situations only last a couple seconds, so one or two dependable actions that are practiced the most, may just be practical lifesavers.

Application

Reaction drills with an attacking partner should begin early in training and continue FOREVER. At first, even though they are simple, and maybe don't require a great deal of technical skill, they are quite important. They redirect instinctive, possible panic reactions, into constructive responses, and de-sensitize students to the idea of a fist coming toward their face. We are conditioned to fear a fist coming at our face, and through training we teach that there are simple alternatives like blocks, redirection, or even just shifting away.

Empowered with Mind-directed Action

The addition of a spirited partner as an opponent into the mix provides essential energy and variables that students learn to cope with as they struggle to use their techniques. Suddenly they are "forced" to respond. Sometimes they do just fine, and sometimes, "Oops!" The more they practice, the more they feel success. If they have a strong foundation of basic skills, success is usually much easier to come by.

The more students study kata *bunkai*, one, three, and five-step-sparring, the more ingrained the use of their karate. Through abundant repetition, students begin to develop mental and physical patterns of correct responses that gradually, over time, become more reflexive. The techniques practiced the most, will be the first to become reflexive and dependable under pressure. The longer the training time, and the richer the experience, the more karate techniques become available for survival. At first everything is a conscious, even a struggling effort, gradually becoming a quicker conscious response, and later evolving into a quickly, nearly automatic response.

Strong Internalization Begins

A stronger core group of fundamental technical skills are becoming internalized to the point that a student is able to perform according to demands and circumstances. Demand might be verbal from and instructor command, an attack in a sparring drill, or even an emergency on the street. Skills may not be refined but they may be fairly strong and workable. One might consider this as the ability of a higher intermediate or advanced level student. More skills are useful and reasonably strong. Students have done repetitive practice for months or years (depending on maturity, enthusiasm, and prior experience) in techniques singly and in combination. They have internalized basics and combinations through more intense *kihon* practice intense study of *kata*. Their use of blocks and counters in basic sparring situations is faster and stronger. Free-sparring and self-defense simulations may be a little clumsy but stronger and the instructor sees more successes. Sparring matches and competition may be introduced so students experience unfamiliar opponents. Students can spar with two or more people at once to intensify sparring as well. The multiple opponents can be placed in front resembling a frontal assault or from different directions to increase mental awareness and technique difficulties. The variety of ways to intensify technique application and mental skill sets is limited only by the imagination of instructors and senior students.

Training is intensified with speed drills, multiple combinations created, faster sparring intensities, increased dynamic kata performance with realistic attacker visualization. An increased emphasis is on the ways to generate power through body connections, expansion and contractions, body core and muscle group uses, driving motions from the floor, and increased focus, *kime*, being increased (power generators covered in another chapter.) Makiwara training or heavy bag training may have been introduced, but now it begins in earnest. All of these will increase mental strengths, result in better physical conditioning, power and effective technique. Success will breed success.

Apprehension of Opponent Intent

Students become more aware of their own space and position in an environment that may be occupied by an opponent. Expanded awareness, "global awareness" is practiced as well as a "focused awareness." Attention to things big and small. This is not to be confused with paranoia. It's just starting to appreciate more of all that is going on around you.

Tactically, gazing becomes important to perceive more. Focus your eyes less to perceive more. *Tsuki no Kokoro*, "mind like the moon," is the ability to see everything. The opponent's tiniest indicators of his intent to attack become more visible, no matter how subtle. It would seem like the vision an eagle might have, flying high over a field until he spies a snake moving in the grass five hundred feet below. Then, he focuses on his victim (lunch) as he dives in for the kill.

Confidence and self-motivation should begin to flourish. *Shugyo*, or austere training, is introduced as something to be valued and enjoyed rather than dreaded. A strong core of basic and dependable karate skill sets is becoming internalized. The karate spirit rises.

Competition, as in tournaments, is helpful and valuable dealing with actions from unknown opponents but is confined to one opponent that you see in front of you. The bigger karate picture is out in the real world, in combat zones, in parking lots at night, in your home or yard while you are preoccupied, and attackers come in multiples from hiding and you must react. Your life may be in the balance.

I know a karateka who came out of a store and was accosted by two would be assailants. Walking to his car, he was blocked in by two bad guys. The middle-aged but strong black belt saw a knife in the hand of the front attacker, and at the same time, noticed another coming up from behind. The front man demanded money. Not really thinking, the black belt threw his grocery sack hard to the front man holding the knife, and front kicked him in the gut at the same time, as hard as possible. The man behind advanced, so he back kicked him in the solar plexus with his shoe heel as hard as possible! Both doubled over gasping, vomiting, and doubled over, ran away. He went back to class and told his sensei, Sensei Randall G. Hassell, "Wow, Sensei! I didn't think about it at the time, but those kicks we practice really worked! Just like in class!"

Sensei Hassell said, "I told him, that's the whole idea!"

Intuitive Response

As clearly an example of the "highest stage" that we hope our training leads to, is a story told by Osamu Ozawa. He came out of a store with bags in hand (sounds like people with shopping bags look like easy targets.) Ozawa was confronted by two bad guys, who it seemed, wanted to steal his car and demanded his keys. In his sixties, Ozawa looked over the too young potential car-jackers as they verbally berated him; they in fact thought he was just a helpless looking little old man with groceries and a nice car. (Never mind that he was from a Japanese family of rich Samurai history, a surviving kamikaze pilot of WWII, and a direct disciple of Gichin Funakoshi) One potential assailant menacingly moved menacingly toward Ozawa. Reflexively, Ozawa Sensei "slapped" him hard in the face with a focused palm-heal strike, crushing his jaw immediately. The young punk crumbled to the pavement, bleeding, moaning and crying out, his jaw crushed kind of sideways. Sensei turned to the other assailant saying, "I've been in karate over fifty-five years. So, if that's okay with you, then..." Waiting around no longer, the other youthful bad guy just turned and ran away at high speed. Later, Sensei admitted that if they had had a gun, it may have turned out differently, but he said did not have time to think, they were close in, empty handed, and underestimated him greatly. He unconsciously exploded into action. The two were later arrested. When the police came, Sensei Ozawa told us he just shrugged his shoulders, and told the police, "I don't know, I just slapped one hard and the other guy ran away!" With increased internalization of karate, the ability to move to react "in one breath" as a response to attack as the masters have agreed upon, becomes a reality.

We all hope to reach these highest stages of karate-do. It has been said historically that, "To win one hundred victories, in one hundred battles, is not the highest skill. But to defeat the enemy without fighting is the highest skill." Of course, training daily in hopes of never having to use violence is our ultimate goal. Training hard makes one feel more secure, quietly confident, and calm.

"Karate is seeing things as they are, not as they seem."

Mentally, this calmness is like *Mizu no Kokoro*, mind like water. In a lake that is serenely calm, reflections are clear and accurate like a mirror. You can see things as they are, NOT what they seem. You not only see the reflections of all above, but you can easily see what is below. In seeing things accurately, you may clearly see ways to avoid trouble. But if there is danger, you quickly, clearly, and more accurately see what needs to be done.

By contrast, if the water is disturbed by waves, dirt and sediment comes to the top, is stirred about, and there is no accurate reflection. Similarly, if your mind is clouded by thoughts of fear, rage, or cluttered with, "What ifs," then you cannot perceive what exactly is in front of you accurately.

The problem in using your thoughts in karate kumite or fighting, is that thinking gets in the way. The intellect is useless; it becomes an obstacle. There is little if any time, for conscious deliberation. Then, the concept of *Mushin*, no mind, becomes more increasingly important.

In the book, *The Unfettered Mind*, Takuan Soho (Zen mentor to Miyamoto Musashi and others) says that after a long period of dedicated practice of the martial arts, "...The function of the intellect disappears...the arms legs and body remember what to do." Only after years of continuous disciplined mental and physical training and practice can these ideal stages be reached.

Learning karate skill sets until they become ingrained into us, part of our being, is our goal. Practicing basics, kata, and a wide variety of kumite and self-defense applications using our skills, gradually moves us toward Nakayama's "Highest Stage." From beginner to expert over a long period of time patiently is a continuing life-long timeline that never ends. As Gichin Funakoshi said, in respect to karate training, "There are no limits."

We have to practice techniques and mental skills until the become second nature; part of us. Practicing basics never ends, Kata makes use of changing directions and performing techniques out of our physical comfort zone. And sparring training in unpredictable situations is useful in training for those times when preplanning anything is impossible. We can improve the odds, but there are no guarantees. Karate training toward those ultimate stages is a journey toward a goal, not a final destination.

CHAPTER 17

Randall G. Hassell:
A Shotokan Legacy

KARATE-DO, as other great endeavors of mankind, may best be known through generations by its legacy in the written word -- definitive evidence of its lasting contribution to humanity. Since its emergence from secrecy, traditional karate has been noted for the talented determined *senseis* who have dedicated their lives to the research, development, and promotion of their martial art.

In this day of overwhelming technological wizardry, we still appreciate the absolute necessity of those rare moments of solitude with a favorite karate book, as we painstakingly search for the perfect technique to reveal itself. We are eager for any spark that ignites inspiration, as we ponder the gravity of a master's words which we pray will trigger our own further understanding. The works that we treasure most offer us unlimited opportunity for contemplation and introspection, as we struggle to use the lessons conveyed by our heroes that help us cope with the challenges of our own lives. They give us both a compass to direct us on the path for own training, according to the heroic standards of the masters, and a window into the essence of *budo*.

If you desire to study *karate-do* more deeply by gaining insight into the thoughts and observations of legends like the late Masatoshi Nakayama, being inspired by the *samurai* journey of ex-kamikaze pilot, Osamu Ozawa, experiencing the adventures of the legendary Stan Schmidt, or widening your perspectives by studying the history and evolution of Shotokan karate-do, then you are no doubt enjoying the works of Randall Hassell. Through his creative and editorial genius, we are able to understand the true nature of some of traditional karate's most respected and notable figures, and to enrich our deep appreciation for our own martial art, through his perspectives on the history and philosophy of Shotokan karate-do.

Randall G. Hassell was a man on a crystal clear and passionate mission. Before his passing, you would have been most apt to find him training and teaching in his role as head task-master in his St. Louis dojo, serving as chief instructor to his beloved American Shotokan Karate Alliance (ASKA) while proudly serving simultaneously as President of the American JKA Karate Association (AJKA), or feverishly hovering at his keyboard, developing some new project. He was in high demand teaching clinics from coast to coast and in the Midwest at our Central Illinois Shotokan Karate Association. He loved teaching all levels of students from beginning youth through experienced black belt instructors.

Hassell wrote, edited, and published over thirty books and literally hundreds of articles and training journals on karate. He was determined and dedicated to communicating information about traditional karate in a way that is both accurate and stimulating. Under his guidance, the ASKA held regular instructor clinics that were taught by other internationally legendary instructors, who included the likes of Osamu Ozawa, Stan Schmidt, Edmond Otis, and James Yabe. Other senior ASKA instructors with decades of training and teaching experience taught regularly as well.

Sensei Randall Hassell was gifted at inspiring excellent karate instructors to share their own thoughts and conclusions with their students; in hopes that those students, in turn, will ponder, examine, debate, and share with each other. This creates a perpetual process necessary for the growth of traditional karate in the future of our modern world.

I was fortunate to spend over twenty-five years being taught, mentored, advised, and in almost daily communication with Sensei Hassell. In all aspects of karate and in writing about karate, he taught me invaluable lessons, and we became very close friends.

A result of his perseverance in polishing his craft to perfection, much like the sword-makers of 16th century Japan, is that his works create a self-perpetuating force - a conduit for knowledge and ideas that serve to strengthen the foundations of *karate-do* for current and future generations.

Randall G. Hassell started karate training in 1960, in St. Louis, Missouri at the age of twelve. "At that time, there was no Shotokan in St. Louis (or, nearly anywhere else in the U.S.)." While informally studying *Matsubayashi Shorin-ryu* and *Goju-ryu* karate with some ex-servicemen who had trained in Okinawa and Japan, he stumbled across the karate textbook, *Karate: The Art of Empty Hand Fighting*, by Nishiyama and Brown. He was so intrigued and fascinated by the beautiful motions of the karate figures and by the authoritative quality of the text, that he wrote a fan letter to Hidetaka Nishiyama in Japan. According to Hassell, "I got my aunt to help me write a letter to Japan because the book said inside, 'Japan Karate Association.' We went to the library to do research in order to find the JKA. I was just a little kid, but I wrote a letter to Mr. Nishiyama in Japan, and he wrote me back. I couldn't believe it! He told me he would be coming back to California in 1961 to teach, and he invited me to come see him. So, I did."

"I was able to go to Mr. Nishiyama's dojo in the summer to train because my parents had relatives in Pasadena, and we traveled there regularly. Sometimes Nishiyama Sensei would teach and sometimes Yutaka Yaguchi Sensei would be teaching. This caused some interesting learning experiences because I had to learn what was being taught at the particular time I was there. For example, the first *kata* I ever learned was

Heian Yondan, because that was what was being taught in the class I could attend, and I learned *Kanku Sho* before *Bassai Dai* and other black belt level *katas.*"

In addition to occasionally attending classes in Master Nishiyama's dojo, Hassell periodically traveled to train with Takayuki Mikami, who arrived in Kansas City, Missouri, in 1964. Then, when Sensei Shojiro Sugiyama came to Chicago, he trained extensively with him, traveling the 300-mile distance between St. Louis and Chicago nearly every weekend in the mid to late-1960s. As an original member of the All-America Karate Federation (AAKF), Hassell was able to bring extremely high caliber instructors to

St. Louis for training, including Hidetaka Nishiyama, Teruyuki Okazaki, Takayuki Mikami, Shojiro Koyama, and even the late Minoru Miyata, who was at that time 9th Dan, a contemporary of Master Nakayama, and the Vice-Chief Instructor of the JKA. Hassell eagerly attended seminars wherever he could find them.

According to Hassell, "The downside of those days was that we didn't have the luxury of a regular instructor in the dojo, that we could just go to for training. The good side was that we had access to many of the best instructors in the world. We were highly motivated and would work feverishly to learn all we possibly could. In 1965, for example, Sugiyama Sensei brought, Taiji Kase, Hirokazu Kanazawa, Hiroshi Shira and Keinosuke Enoeda to Chicago. In 1968, Nakayama Sensei himself came to teach us, and we soaked it up like a sponge."

Randall Hassell's writing career began in the early 70s by assisting the AAKF in the writing of manuals and public relations projects. His articles appeared often in magazines in those days, in the likes of *Kick Illustrated, Inside Karate, Karate Illustrated*, and in *Black Belt* magazine, where his regular monthly column, titled "The Karate Spirit", appeared for over three years. Since the mid-1980s he has concentrated on books and had written, co-authored, and been a major contributor, or editor, or publisher for more than 30 major traditional karate books, journals and manuals. He founded Focus Publications, which was a major martial art publishing company for 15 years. Three of his works, which will no doubt have lasting popularity, and have made major contributions to traditional karate, are *Samurai Journey, Conversations with the Master: Masatoshi Nakayama*, and *Shotokan Karate: Its History and Evolution*.

Samurai Journey is the spectacular life story of Osamu Ozawa. It is a story of human triumph over impossible odds. Ozawa began his own samurai journey as a kamikaze pilot who survived his suicide plane's crash on take-off to his intended final flight into destiny. He spent months hospitalized with his limbs bandaged and in traction to heal his broken body, when many his friends committed suicide at their country's surrender, only to return to his devastated home several weeks after his own funeral had been conducted!

Ozawa's story portrays his triumphant rise to stardom as a highly successful television director, his major role in the original development of the Japan Karate Association (JKA), his travels to the U.S. and South America to teach karate, and the like. He rose to the heights of being a multi-millionaire several times, only to tumble to the depths of despair and poverty. His bravery against impossible odds is a credit to his *samurai* heritage and an inspiration to us all.

According to Hassell "The story of Master Ozawa is too amazing to be fiction. It is a remarkable story with so many twists of fate, coincidences, and quirky events that this man lived through that had a tremendous impact on his life. I had known him for almost fifteen years and had listened to his stories many times before he asked me to write this book. It took me six years to write it, and I'm still amazed at his life. The unique thing about Ozawa Sensei to me, was that he was the most readily accessible Japanese instructor I've ever met. He seemed to me to have a genuine emotional connection with people. I find it remarkable that he never hesitated, even once, to tell me deeply personal and painful things that happened to him in his life."

Another master with whom Randall Hassell's name has been intimately associated is Masatoshi Nakayama, one of the most celebrated instructors of this century. Nakayama has been often credited for the worldwide introduction and global popularity of Shotokan karate-do, and for virtually inventing the concept of organized sport karate. He was one of Master Funakoshi's senior disciples and for decades was the Chief Instructor of the Japan Karate Association. As head of the JKA, Master Nakayama was at the helm of the organization which, at that time, had developed some of the most technically proficient karate men the world had ever seen, and sent them from their homeland to publicly spread karate throughout the world. He wrote more than twenty books on karate-do, which are considered to be standard reference for serious Shotokan karate-ka. He will forever be an icon of leadership in the history of martial arts, a standard by which others are measured.

In the early 1980s, Randall Hassell wrote *Conversations with The Master: Masatoshi Nakayama*, a compilation of the most complete and comprehensive interviews that Master Nakayama ever granted to a Western journalist. This book portrays the history and philosophy of Nakayama Sensei in his own words. It is a window of insight into the very essence and spirit of karate-do.

According to Hassell, Nakayama Sensei's superior leadership enabled the JKA to be as successful as it was. After spending much time with Master Nakayama, Hassell found the highly revered sensei's personality to be very frank and straightforward, although reserved. He also found Nakayama

Sensei to be incredibly humble, sincere, very down-to-earth, and able to relate to people at every level of society.

"When I interviewed him, he was in his late sixties, at the pinnacle of the JKA. It was the largest single-style karate organization in the world, unified under his leadership. One time in Denver, just before one of our interview sessions, my eight year-old son and I were watching him teach a black belt clinic. He had a steely-eyed look about him. He was really being extremely firm and strong with these young black belts, pushing them very hard, again and again, literally knocking them around, breaking their stances, and so on. As the class ended, my son fell down and pinched his finger on a chair and started crying. As he came off the floor, Nakayama saw my son crying and instantly switched his stern expression into one of compassion. As it happened, he had just recently seen the movie *E.T.*, where E.T. points his finger out to heal wounds. Master Nakayama stopped, surrounded by Yaguchi Sensei and many sweating black belts, and he tenderly put his finger out to my son and said in his best E.T. voice, "Ouch, ouch, I fix! I fix! Ouch!" Then he patted my son gently and got him laughing. It was such a touching and kind thing that he did, but that's the way he was. I think that illustrates the very essence of Nakayama as a person, as I knew him. He was genuinely humane, interested, and sensitive. He was a very nice man, and yet, one of the strongest karate men the world has ever seen."

The work of Randall Hassell is not only important because of the colorful biographic portrayals of important key figures and their contributions to karate-do, but also because of his unique ability to bring out the power in their personalities that propels them to phenomenal heights of leadership.

Stan Schmidt is such a figure. He was the first non-Japanese ever to be granted the title of *Shihan* by the Japan Karate Association. Shihan literally means " a model for the rest" and is a title legitimately reserved for very few. At that time, Schmidt was seventh *Dan* and chief instructor of the South Africa JKA. He is living proof, after more than thirty training trips to Japan, that a Westerner can train with the Japanese instructors on their own terms and succeed. His creative genius, expressed in Hollywood movies, inspirational training videos, and books, along with his infectious positive attitude and his karate skills, are legendary. His steel, tested by a near-fatal car crash that resulted in double hip replacement surgeries, held strong during his near-miraculous recovery and return to both karate training and teaching.

Randall Hassell worked with him as editor, encourager, and publisher on three books, *Recognition* (a novel*)*, *Spirit of the Empty Hand*, and *Meeting Myself; Beyond Spirit of the Empty Hand*, and on numerous DVDs. According to Sensei Schmidt, "I'm so pleased that Mr. Hassell kept encouraging me. When one is in a weakened state, other strengths, usually the spiritual strengths, come to the surface. I've experienced certain things that others can use as a platform to better themselves. By reading my books, I hope others can be inspired to go to further heights."

Randall Hassell had worked very closely with Stan Schmidt as editor and publisher for years leading up to the publication of *Meeting Myself: Beyond Spirit of the Empty Hand*, with his second publishing company, Damashi Publications. This book portrays Schmidt's early days of training in Japan, through his nearly miraculous comeback from a nearly fatal car crash. Asked about his impressions from working with Sensei Schmidt, Hassell comments, "He is one of the best representations of what traditional karate can do for people physically, psychologically, and spiritually. After two hip replacements, he is still one of the strongest karate men in the world. And I think one of Stan Schmidt's biggest contributions to worldwide karate-do will be in empowering people to regain control of their lives, especially after a personal crisis, utilizing their training in karate-do to move forward, regardless of their physical condition. People, who have been training in karate and *budo* for a long time, feel like they are in control of their own space. When something bad happens or they age and have injuries, illnesses, or surgeries, for example, they may feel like they are losing that control. They may feel that life itself has gone out of control and has been taken away. I think that Stan Schmidt has proven that this is only an illusion. He has clearly demonstrated that if they can move their bodies at all, they can still progress. This is an immeasurable contribution that empowers people to regain command of their own lives."

Of the 100 or so magazine articles that Randall Hassell has written, one "got out of hand," he says, and resulted in a full-blown, definitive text on the history of Shotokan. He had written an article on Shotokan history for *Kick Illustrated* which peaked enough interest to become a four-part series. Because of a keen interest in his own roots in karate, and because he had been able to spend an incredible amount of time around Masters Nakayama, Nishiyama, Okazaki, Mikami, Sugiyama, and the like, he had been able to gather a great deal of valuable first-hand information. After doing additional research and more information gathering, he published *Shotokan Karate: Its History and Evolution*, the first authoritative and comprehensive history text on Shotokan karate-do. This book was well received by karate people around the world, has had at least eight printings.

In the early 90s, Randall Hassell, Rick Brewer, Carl Hartter, met together in Las Vegas, and planned and founded the American Shotokan Karate Alliance (ASKA.) "We believe," Hassell said, "that the term 'alliance' clearly expresses our intentions regarding the development of traditional Shotokan karate-do. We now have many alliances and friendships with national and international organizations that have a similar purpose. The term 'alliance' means that we share common goals and mutual recognition and support, but we don't interfere with each other's organizational business."

As a perfect example of friendships, cooperation, and mutual support, Randall Hassell and Edmond Otis co-authored the very comprehensive, informative, and entertaining book, *The Complete Idiots Guide to Karate*, that was published by Macmillan. This book had been published in at least three languages and sold world-wide. Both men were firmly committed to the spirit of sharing and cooperation that fosters the growth and well-being of karate students, and the future quality and advancement of Shotokan karate.

Regardless of any past organizational differences that Randall Hassell and others may have historically had with the past JKA structure, he never displayed animosity, only admiration and appreciation. To the contrary, he had an absolute, utmost respect for the Japanese and all aspects of their convention and ethics related to traditional karate-do.

In Hassell's opinion, "The masters, who, by their own initiative, left their homelands to share their wealth of knowledge with the world, should be appreciated as international treasures. These senior Japanese instructors, who were taught directly by Master Funakoshi and his peers, and who left their families often traveling penniless to countries of vastly foreign cultures and languages in order to teach karate, deeply deserve our gratitude and respect. Through their determined efforts and their own raw courage, they have positively influenced and changed the lives of millions of people around the world. This, I believe, will be their lasting legacy."

And what did Randall G. Hassell want his own legacy to be? "My students, of course, are the products of my best efforts, and I hope they keep on training and pass on their karate to others."

The works of Randall Hassell represent much more than the product of a few brief interviews with popular celebrity instructors. They represent literally thousands of hours of thoughtful and insightful sharing by great men in their quiet moments - men who are extraordinary in their contributions to humanity through this beautiful martial art. These are masters of *budo* in every way, who would have instantly sensed any false intentions or hypocrisy from their interviewer. Indeed, they must have sensed only absolutely sincere dedication. As a result of his skills, "pen and sword in accord," Randall Hassell Sensei has succeeded in creating a conduit for the rest of us, so that we are able to glimpse into the hearts of men who represent the generation of senior masters who graciously introduced Master Funakoshi's karate-do to the world.

CHAPTER 18

Wrong Impressions: Prejudice is Weakness

Webster defines prejudice as "preconceived judgement or opinions...or an opinion based on non-objectivity." Non-objectivity is the opposite as seeing things as they really ARE. This is weakness in karate.

CLEAR THINKING and objectivity are hallmarks of karate-do. In martial arts terms, preconceived judgements can be disastrous; you draw conclusions prematurely and get easily deceived by an opponent. You may size up your opponent to be an old, harmless weakling, but you did not notice the callouses on his knuckles. Or maybe at the last minute he pulls out a concealed 45 automatic. Or perhaps has three friends hiding who jump out of the shadows. Remember that karate training is about "seeing things as they really are; NOT what they SEEM." Clearly, making premature judgements on first impressions or appearances is bad; a weakness of character or a subconscious tendency that must be weeded out. Traditional karate demands "the beginners mind," because we are constantly learning, reflecting, and we are a work in progress. Drawing conclusions by such faulty thinking is tactically dangerous.

The bigger reality of prejudice on a huge mind-boggling scale, is a dark and ugly shadow. It is a poor statement on the progress of mankind that even now it is a stain on humanity. Having unfounded prejudice demonstrates ignorance, and human ugliness in an inexcusable form. In social prejudicial contagion, others join in, and the victims, who have been labeled artificially "different," suffer needless cruelty.

Tyrants and dictators throughout recent and ancient history use perceived differences in people to blame, to gain power, and in order to manipulate others with the use faulty perceptions. Genocide is an extreme and all too frequent example that reoccurs and hides beneath a thin vail of civility.

Well known examples are Hitler murdering 6 million people, institutionalized Apartheid in South Africa, tribal and religious genocides in Eastern Europe, Rwanda and other African nations, genocide against our Native Americans, slavery and crimes against Black Americans litter history. Nations, religion, skin color, gender, general dress, appearance, neighborhoods, and the like, still cause people to judge irrationally with horrifying results. These, sadly, are but a few and more memorably infamous.

Even small subtle prejudging tendencies, often unknown to the afflicted individual, can unconsciously cause bad common-sense decision making. Let's look at some almost humorous assumptions, but potentially dangerous illustrations: All salesmen have your best interest at heart? A friendly phone voice tells you that you have won the Sweepstakes so you tell them your social security number and send them $500 just to hold it for you!...hmmm. Perhaps you visit a friend to see his new pistol and assume that it was unloaded because it is on his coffee table: not safe, not smart. You assume all gray-haired guys with ragged gray karate belts are old and slow…this could really get you some bruises. You may assume that since you live in the rural countryside, that you do not have to lock your doors…and your family and your stuff will be safe…this could get you robbed and dead.

I am not saying that accurate assessments and judgments calls cannot be made by sizing up situations, objectively, and ahead of time to determine a course of action. That is why we have to develop accurate and quick "judgment abilities" in combat. In karate we train at observation and awareness skills. Correct and swift judgments are made by objectively evaluating behaviors and actions…not by prejudice.

Often, we look someone over quickly and assume they will be a certain way. In training, if you want to test this out, simply face your opponent and decide, ahead of the fact, what he is going to do. That is, pre-judge his attack and prepare for just that attack. Feel lucky! Simple enough, now according to your guess, get your best block-counter ready, and execute them as soon as your partner moves. No changing your mind. OOPS! You decided (ahead of time) that your opponent was going to kick to your gut, but instead, a flurry of punches explode in your face.

In authentic karate-do, Funakoshi his peers and his students express a strong sense of social justice in the behavior and judgement of serious karate-do students. The idea of prejudice has caused great misery throughout human history and shows little sign that humans have progressed beyond this basic tendency. But at least karate-do studies assume that we are all a work in progress and offers hope in sternly assigning each participant to continually make great individual effort at improving character on the side of justice and making positive contributions to society. Karate is more mental growth and more mental strength than physical. The good guys must be strong.

The best posture is to assume nothing, prejudge nothing, keep your eyes open and your mind clear, react to what comes, not to what you think might come. See things as they are, not what they might at first glance seem.

Applied Dojo Kun

The first rule of conduct outlined in Funakoshi's *Dojo Kun* (Dojo Code) is to strive for perfection of character." This rules out making stupid, hurtful premature judgments about humanity for superficial reasons (prejudicial behaviors).

Strategically, and tactically, prejudice easily results in your defeat in training, and injury and possibly your death in combat. Assuming and prejudging is a weakness you must try to root out. It is an EASY opening for your opponent to use against you. Masters throughout the history of human conflict, large and small, stress that must live in the "now." React and observe only what "is" and you will be more successful. If you are easily prejudiced, then your opponent can cause you to misjudge, then you are easily tricked, misled, and set up by your opponent to be his victim.

Lack of prejudice is a good moral and ethical quality to create harmony among humans; part of striving for "perfection of character." Be aware of only real threats and to react to them appropriately. Avoid predispositions that can cause your own destruction.

If you realize you have prejudices, open your mind and let them go. Throw them away.

Here is a true and actually a humorous demonstration…just food for thought: One of my young black belts fought in a tournament. Looking across at his opponent he was facing an older man, with thinning gray hair, a nearly white rag for a black belt. My young *Shodan* assumed right away that he was an old slow guy, someone that should be an easy win. The ref said, "*Hajime!*" One second later, WHAM! A foot sweep and a punch ended the match, with my young warrior on his backside on the floor…

"*Ippon!*" My student told me later that he should have known better. The old guy with the gray thinning hair and ragged belt had secret weapons: experience and wisdom. He learned a fast lesson about prejudging people and opponents on appearances, first impressions, and about how hard a floor landing can be on one's backside!

CHAPTER 19

Mediocrity is Unacceptable: The Stakes Are Just Too High

THE FIRST GENERATION of Japanese masters to introduce karate to the West, and indeed the world, will be a hard act to follow. But even more challenging than the karate training they offered, is that history is passing the baton, the future development of karate along to all of us.

Some years ago, we hosted Master Osamu Ozawa for numerous clinics around Central Illinois, St. Louis, and St. Charles, Missouri. He was a fascinating link to karate history; his classes were challenging, incredibly valuable, and his real-life stories were riveting.

Ozawa Sensei loved to reminisce about his early training experiences with Funakoshi, and told us how he, Nakayama Sensei, and many other great instructors struggled to bring karate to the forefront of public recognition with credibility. He shared that karate was not always welcome by everyone in post-World War II Japan, and he showed the sword-attack scars on his forearms to prove it. But like Funakoshi, these great men were convinced that karate was a powerful force for ethical human improvement worldwide.

"No matter who you are or where you come from," Ozawa said, "because we all sweat together on the dojo floor, and are all working on the same goals, we become friends."

Inspired, I had written a couple articles featuring some of Ozawa's shared thoughts and perspectives. I was so surprised when I received a very unique "Thank You" letter. In it, he told me that karate could potentially be of "benefit to millions of Americans." Then, he said, "American karate must be taken care of by Americans," who would have a better understanding of how that might be accomplished. He closed with what seemed a rather cryptic, thought-provoking admission. Master Ozawa ended with:

"Our generation almost finishing. Sincerely, Osamu Ozawa"

Ozawa Sensei is one of the generations of Japanese masters who brought Karate to the West. He said that the future of karate in the West is now up to us: clearly laying the challenge and the responsibility at our feet.

Mediocrity is never a gold standard for student performance. Karate equips students with dramatic new skill sets and ways to dig deeply, teaches them to draw upon their own human potentials critically needed life and death situations. As for instructors, the same level of excellence that we hope for, or demand from our students, should be reflected in the quality and effort we put in our teaching. If you demand quality teaching performance of yourself, then it will certainly show in your students. Your students are a mirror of your own teaching ability. Some, no doubt, will become the very instructors who will carry on the legacy started by our Japanese instructors, or in the words of Funakoshi, they will "pass it along straight and well."

Below is a poem that I purposely put at the front of this book to set a tone. It was quite unexpectedly originally published some years ago, halfway around the world from me, in the legendary Stan Schmidt's, *S.A. JKA TODAY*, his South African JKA Karate Association Members Magazine. It illuminates the purpose, responsibility, and potential of being a traditional karate sensei.

A Word, a Spark, a Blaze

Even the slightest well-aimed word
    May ignite a life-long passion for karate,
But teaching karate is like keeping kindling aglow
    During a mountain blizzard ---
If instructors fan too briskly, without proper focus,
   void of purpose,
    They may clumsily scatter the sparks to the wind.
The challenge then, is to nurture and temper,
   inspire and lead,
    Fan the desire to learn karate, until it becomes a self-sustaining blaze!

By Author

Mediocrity is not acceptable. The stakes are too high.

To insure a robust, credible, long-term future for karate, it must be taught in a highly effective, productive, and professional manner. Mediocrity is not acceptable. The stakes are too high. Both the quality of students who will determine the future of karate, and the legacy of the generation of tremendously dedicated instructors, who came to the West to introduce karate to the world, are at stake.

CHAPTER 20

Commitment is Power!

FOR HUNDREDS, even thousands of years, before it had a name, the necessity for training in fighting skills was paramount in human evolution. Whether bare-handed or with weapons, the commitment to fighting for survival was occupational; for the right just to live.

And while we live under a great veil of civility, much has not changed. One important rule, yes rule, I remind myself repeatedly of (and it appears as a survival component in other contexts in my writing) is that in karate, is we MUST see things as they really are. Civilization offers a wonderful structure for living with hope, security, freedom, progress, and the like; but unfortunately, the wolves still get hungry. In any media, you can watch faith, hope, and charity: the best of human nature. But with the mere touch of a finger, you can switch to view pure and endless barbarism.

As I first wrote this, we in the US had two domestic terrorism incidents over one weekend, with dozens brutally murdered and many more critically wounded; just because of racism and insanity. The commitment to survivability, is just as important as when we first came out of the caves.

As important as karate training is to many of us, given the daily grind of modern life, it takes commitment to regularly set aside the time and energy to train as we would like. It is so important and rewarding to adopt karate as a lifestyle (karate-do) so that training just becomes part of who you are. Training intensity will come and go, ebb and flow, it will adjust to life's necessities, but it can always be there even as you get older.

I often have students who feel guilty as some life crisis causes them to take time off. I reassure them that if you assume the karate "way," all is well, and that karate is only as far away as their thoughts. In fact, Karate may assist them and give them strength to face whatever challenges they have to face. I've never charged enough for karate to live on so high school teaching was my "day job" to support my family, make the bills, and of course to help my karate expenses. Stan Schmidt once told me that karate was my real job and teaching in the public high school was just my occupation to support my karate. Very true. High school was extremely challenging day to day; as I taught career education to some talented kids, some students with special needs, some delinquents, and all well overdosed on teenage hormones! The physical eye-hand skills I taught to Technical Education students reinforced all teaching I did in karate eye-hand technique. The understanding of how people learned and reacted under pressure in Karate classes helped my daytime high school classes. Karate was so very refreshing because my karate students wanted to learn as much karate as they could like sponges! By contrast, my daily high school student clients had to be in attendance whether they wanted to or not. Karate was so VERY much more fun.

A couple times I received job promotions that required extra day, night, and weekend work just to keep up. When I would begin to feel the stress of my high school teaching job, budgets, discipline problems, etc., I would always turn to my karate for strength and perspective.

Karate gave me stress management, fitness, confidence, clear thinking, and words of encouragement, including great peer support to charge my batteries. I loved the process of teaching in the high school, shaping lives, teaching career survival, and character improvement to my high school students. And in karate, same process in a different way. I was the only teacher in Pekin Community High School that had Funakoshi's Dojo Kun posted in his room. Those were usually great topics for questions and discussions.

Our great *budo* masters were incredibly principle driven. By design, the character strengths and qualities built in the dojo for karate improvement can be directly applied to improve our everyday lives as well. One of my favorite quotes attributed to Gichin Funakoshi, "Karate is like boiling water; if not given continuous heat, it will soon become cold" is about the need for continuity, determination, and commitment.

By developing the commitment needed to continue training, you empower yourself to reap short term benefits (defending against attack) and long-term benefits (physical and psychological well-being). It pays dividends.

Most people, however, cannot comprehend studying one thing at a time for very long with the goal of its perfection. Lay people often are awed, observing even a fairly skilled karate student performing a good basic kata. They stare with mouths agape at a work of fine art. They jump with glee when their favorite baseball player hits a home run. Instead of a sideline sport, karate is all about participation with continuous positive rewards, small and large.

"The effects of karate are cumulative."

The great mystery of seemingly superhuman feats of all sorts are hidden in plain sight. Even average people can perform exceptionally well if they would only study a thing continuously. As Funakoshi said, "The effects of karate are cumulative." So, even if you can only train a few minutes a day, do it. Your hard-earned karate skills will thrive. Even If you are laid up in a hospital then think about it. Sparring tactics are fun to visualize and you can always win! Visualization is a powerful technique that all Olympians and professional athletes use.

Stan Schmidt often tells his own story lying in the hospital after a serious car accident, wondering if he would ever be able to train again. When he felt he had hit rock bottom, he began striking a flat rock with his fist, one punch, one thud at a time. Weakly at first, but gradually with more conviction, his fighting spirit and then his strength slowly returned. His power of commitment, already legendary in Karate, brought him back from personal tragedy.

When he first told us his story, I thought, "Wow! What a personal karate comeback." But many years, two hip replacements, and a couple bouts with cancer in my own life, I understood all too well! And I will not bore the reader, but I use this story my own personal way.

In every example I've used, the most crucial, common, redeeming behavioral component to evading or conquering problems of all sorts is commitment.

Don't be surprised if, as you watch many people around you set themselves up for failure, you immediately see lack of commitment. Musashi and other sword masters said that when you attack, you must commit to a feeling of crashing into your opponent's body with your own so that your cut is decisive, and you break through your opponent's defense to cut him down.

This is committing all of your courage and energy toward a goal, but in this case, also ignoring your own doubts to move forward. Going in halfway and changing your mind would get you killed. The power if commitment is a resource within you to draw from. Commitment is like planting a spring corn crop over miles of fields. After you start planting, your see nothing but dirt. Then a little green appears, and before long corn plants can tower over your head. It can start slowly and reap great lasting rewards.

One popular old Samurai expression is, "When you are afraid, tense your belly and attack!"

I tell my own students to think of driving into their opponent's space like a Federal Express truck to "deliver" your attack. This is commitment. Lack of it will set you up for repeated failure in all aspects of your life. I read somewhere that Abraham Lincoln lost seven elections on his way to becoming one of our greatest presidents. But he kept trying over and over — a man on a mission. You will succeed at making yourself miserable, and not accomplishing many, many things that are well within your abilities and intelligence, without a little commitment. You will always fall short of your best effort, and you will know it. In terms of karate-do and martial arts, lack of purpose and conviction lowers your daily training expectations and your acquired martial arts skill. You will allow yourself to approach training half-heartedly, and your results will be lackluster. Hesitating in fighting or kumite, or life in general, can repeatedly cause you frustrating failures — grief that you bring upon yourself by selling yourself short.

Commitment is often a slow and low-key continued process, like a diet or other change in habit or behavior. But it can also be a power switch that you learn to flip on for extreme measures to be taken instantly in time of need. It is a great and dependable source of success!

CHAPTER 21

Success:
Preparation Encounters Demand

SKILLED CARPENTERS can build with knowledge, tools, and strategies; calmly adjusting as changes are needed, accomplishing goals and breeding successes. They begin with basic skills learned, perhaps through the more detailed preparation in technical schools and apprenticeships, have on-the-job training to apply these skills under the guidance of more seasoned craftspeople, until they become skilled problem solvers construction experts who can work wonders! Musashi often used similar analogies in his writings as "formulas" for success in life and mortal combat. The same is true with karate. We must learn all that is possible to learn, train correctly day after day, and use this preparation to guide our actions as the direct result of accumulated and dedicated training. We cannot become easily flustered by unsuspected twists and turns. We must work toward calmly perceiving threats, and accurately dealing with what comes our way. Granted, what comes our way can be in the form of life-challenges that we may dread, or in the form of sudden emergencies of the world we find ourselves, and of course, in the form of surprise physical assault that requires our direct applications of karate skill.

If you study famous warrior strategies throughout history, you find their ideas for confronting great challenges in other arenas like politics, business, and international relations, etc. I found Musashi's *Book of Five Rings* for sale in the business section of a store on Michigan Avenue's, Gold Coast, in Chicago. His strategies are respected in competitive business practices, just as in karate practices. They are applicable for armies, companies, and individuals alike. Preparation is a universal necessity for success.

The blunt old-fashioned samurai outlook comes from pretty much from one mindset: you live, or you die. Training, commitment, and an unassailable fighting spirit can determine outcomes.

Osamu Ozawa Sensei, a direct student of Gichin Funakoshi, often stressed that whether in dojo training, or in tournament competition, we control our distance so that practice and competitions are safe. However, he adamantly stressed that in our practice, our spirit should show the strong "intent to hit them!" That way, students know what it feels like to be faced with a terrifying aggressor to prepare them to use their karate training to save their life on the street. Training is safe, but intensity is critical preparation!

Just this past summer we hosted a camp featuring Minoru Kawawada, the Chief Instructor of Nakayama's famed Hoitsugan Dojo in Tokyo. Kawawada sensei warned us not to "kid ourselves" about our karate. He taught that, Karate is Budo, and said, "If you don't practice your basics and kata like you are in a fight, it will not work when you need it!"

Correct preparation is critical because you will get what you practice. In karate, we train the mind and body to work together. We do this, so we can direct our techniques and movements at will, with minimal hesitation, and to maximize our human potentials. Training poorly does not lead to success. Being dilligent about teaching students to perform techniques appropriately must be a hallmark of our classes. Otherwise, misguided energy leads to wasted time, poor results, and ineffective skill sets that are not dependable when we need them the most. High quality training is the reliable path to effective actions. Literally, your life may depend on your preparation.

The importance of quality training is that the mind unconsciously directs the body to move in the manner we have trained to move. Training is like downloading software into your laptop. The better the input, the better output! Success is when preparation meets opportunity in a tournament. More importantly, in life threatening circumstances, success may be your preparation meeting demands that literally, your life may depend upon.

CHAPTER 22

Highly Effective Karate Teaching Empowering Toward the Higher Stages

You Need to Know Where You Are Going, in Order to Get There!

THIS CHAPTER is a small excerpt of a book I wrote to help karate instructor development for my advanced students who wish to become good karate instructors in the future. And it's also a guide and trouble-shooting text for those, who want to double check on our own teaching methods and fine tune for better student success. Some students pick things up quickly, and some, no matter how hard they try are challenging. We all have surprising success stories that inspire us to teach. There are those success stories that bring joy. I had one student who came into the dojo to bring her boys into class. She came in using canes for balance and faithfully watched from a chair as her boys trained. After a short time, she wanted to try it out too. We urged her to just enjoy the learning karate. It wasn't long and she didn't need canes as stance training brought new strength, and then she progressed to intermediate levels of skills that brought great satisfaction and joy to all of my teaching staff.

I've always been inspired by a quote attributed to the legendary Japanese sword master, Miyamoto Musashi, that as one would guess, gets right to the point!

"Do nothing that is without purpose."

Keep in mind that the purpose determines what you need to do. Some instructors have a knack for being goal oriented, looking ahead in their thinking, and are able to dream up the needed activities and skill sets to help students achieve goals.

It's kind of like using a "Karate Teaching GPS." Don't worry if you don't feel that this comes easily to you. If you need to, you can simply write the outcomes you want for your student(s) and then sketch out the steps or drills you need to put students through. Some students learn in leaps! Some learn in baby steps.

Know the purpose of every lesson.

It's pretty natural for new assistant instructors to think they are modeling their instructors by lining everyone up and counting at the top of their lungs. That's probably because the great instructors they are modeling make teaching karate look easy - from the sideline. And the very first time your instructor asks you to step out front and take over class can be a super "Light-bulb moment" for you. Starting to form habits of having even a small goal for each lesson and accomplishing it, will build your confidence and increase your student's success. (Of course, if your goal is just to make them sweat, count away!)

As for Musashi's emphasis on having purpose: I think that excellent teaching and proper instructor leadership are like taking your students on an expedition through a dense jungle. Even mediocre instructors can teach their students how to effectively swing a machete to cut a path. In fact, given minimum instruction, smarter students can figure out efficient knife-flailing, slicing, and dicing techniques all on their own. Gifted students can teach themselves. But to be a highly effective karate instructor, it is our job to regularly "climb that tree" to ensure that we and our students are going in the right direction!

It is incredibly important as a karateka, teaching or in training, to define goals, small and large, and then teach toward them, having a clear vision of the purpose.

Here are a few generally helpful hints to ease the process: to establish main priorities and what you intend to accomplish. Here is some food for thought to trigger teaching and end-game ideas.

Think of the big picture; that traditional karate programs are for long-term, life-style benefits (Karate-do/Budo). Consequently, this includes creating diverse lessons for training all ages and abilities. Break big lessons and big skills down into smaller bits and hammer away building the pieces. Then, as small skills are accomplished, start gluing them back together to assemble bigger goals. This is just how humans learn best. Each person is different so figure different ways for them to get to the same place. All people learn better through some learning channels than others. Some learn by seeing a demonstration. Some learn by going through and trying techniques on each other in a tactile mode. Some learn by hearing an explanation. If you are teaching to a group, the best instructors teach by demonstrating while incorporating as many learning channels into a lesson as possible. Karate is a wonderful activity for incorporating unlimited ways to reach so many different channels. Conversely, this is why karate can benefit so many of our human senses as we say we learn it through mind and body: because we really are.

Lessons and purposes must be individualized for different groups of students, and yet, the goal of black belt levels may be the same for all. Kata, self-defense, competition, rank tests, as part of your program, are incorporated into short and long-term enhanced lessons. They all bring realism and a sense of urgency to training; motivation and enthusiasm! Adjust and form new desired skill sets and goals regularly. Effective teaching is work. We must monitor student progress and change directions to accommodate needs, abilities, injury, talent, and even home environment. We are always keeping our teaching goals in mind. Again, it's like climbing that jungle tree to make sure we are going in the right direction. Teaching is always learning. That is why we all have to keep "the beginner's mind."

This is hardly scratching the surface of "doing nothing without purpose." Work on developing goals while keeping your student progress and priorities in focus. This keeps you pointed in the right direction when you make your drills, classes, practices, and training strategies, etc. Then, within your overall goals, develop specific "action-plans" and activities for short term and long-range goals. Make your Karate Teaching GPS, and then your students will reach goals developing at their own best. If you keep these considerations in mind, you will be a very effective karate instructor. By challenging so many components of a human being, and improving, it only makes sense that we feel so much satisfaction learning and teaching karate! Students continually realize their goals. As a teacher, you must simply know where you wish to take them before you miraculously get there. Karate-do is an exceptional vehicle to make better human beings.

CHAPTER 23

Avoiding Violence

MASATOSHI NAKAYAMA was quoted as saying that if any karate technique is used unjustly in violent behavior, then it is not in any way a true karate technique. Nakayama Sensei condemned any use of karate for violence. Osamu Ozawa, spoke from the background of a Samurai family tradition in Japan, of a kamikaze pilot, and a karateka who was attacked by blade wielding assassins, just for promoting karate in the early days in Japan. Ozawa was also a direct student of Gichin Funakoshi, and he proudly condemned violence, professing that "All violence is bad!"

At a YWCA where I teach, they have "A Week Without Violence" every year.

We teach in every karate class for all ages that every week should be nonviolent. We see no contradiction at all; on the contrary. During the official week without violence, we feel quite proud to study the true purpose of Shotokan karate: the perfection of character of the practitioner.

The karate "codes of behavior," or *Dojo Kun*, in traditional karate most always contain a mention of restraining from having a bad temper, losing self-control, refraining from impetuous behavior, etc. Constructive attitudes are an important part of traditional karate and of course, as karate-do was introduced to the wider world, the masters didn't want karate to be misunderstood as just a violent activity with no redeeming values. One really fascinating thing in karate is that philosophical things are usually double-edged swords with practical, strategic, and often highly critical purposes. In other words, karate's seemingly idealistic platitudes also have extremely practical applications "where the rubber meets the road!"

Karate training is learning to see how things around us, perceptions and points of view, not to mention potentially dangerous situations, really are. This is important to employing strategies and tactics: having a clear perceptive mind and not misjudging situations so we may react correctly. It's a tall order to fill, however your life may depend on it in real-world application. Remarkably, karate training is all about trying to perfect things that can never be perfected: but with practice, we improve, we get closer.

Karate is striving to perfect things that can never be perfected.

Guarding against impetuous behavior or controlling your temperament in karate is kind of like saying look before you leap, so that you don't do anything stupid, unnecessarily violent, or even self-destructive, in a mine field of possibilities. Impetuousness, impulsiveness, blind rage and behavior derived from prejudice, are dangerous on many levels. Historically on a grand scale, the human race has a bad record on handling these impulses. Humans are responsible for mayhem ranging from road rage all the way to genocide. Karate-do is a powerful medium for learning to step back, maybe cool off and re-access situations, and work on conquering personal impulsive weakness. It's a package deal as a lifestyle that has philosophic, character building, practical, strategic, and tactical values. Lessons certainly come from the words and literature of great karate masters, but wonderfully, often many lessons come to us from the dojo floor. Making good judgements from acute awareness is ideal. But, if we are in the habit making assumptions in sparring for example, we can easily be deceived and baited. If too impetuous, we can be led into our opponent's traps. Much emphasis is placed on staying calm, open minded, and sizing up situations accurately: in real time, instant by instant, in milliseconds. Losing perspective with a bad temper (road rage?) or making premature impulsive mistakes that we regret is just plain dangerous.

Impetuous behavior can cause a "bull in the china shop syndrome." Risking action without thinking, with anger, prejudice, or impetuousness, is a dangerous and self-destructive way to proceed. Avoiding violence is an everyday job!

CHAPTER 24

Makiwara: The Force Be From You!

I CAN THINK OF FEW PIECES of training equipment that is the Hallmark of an endeavor's spirit than the makiwara does in karate. Think about it. The punching post has an immoveable posture, to test our mental tenacity and mental focus and simultaneously our karate technique components interacting, with the makiwara is a brutally honest process. It is a blunt teacher. It does not falter in letting us know our weak points. But still, it lets us appreciate our strong points. If you train with the makiwara long, you know what I mean. Google "Fans of Makiwara Training," you will quickly find thousands of like-minded Budoka who feel the joy of hammering on this very old and reliable friend!

The makiwara replaces an actual opponent. You may make the mistake of thinking it's just standing there and can't hurt you if you get lax using it: you would be wrong. Unlike practicing in the air without an opponent, it refuses to allow you to be indifferent under any circumstances. Karate is a form of Budo, and the punching post becomes an irreplaceable teacher. It hammers your mental and physical steel like a blacksmith forges a blade. You may be a quick learner when it comes to the movements of hundreds of karate techniques. But, your makiwara will surely teach you to fully comprehend the real value of each. This is critical for understanding which are most effective for actual use, and which are not, so that you are stronger and less vulnerable.

Karate is known for developing impact shock waves — kinetic energy. The destructive forces in technique are more like a speeding race car than a bulldozer. No matter the size of the serious karate student, the science behind the creation of the destructive shock waves work. The general formula for creating karate energy is E=1/2 Mass times Velocity (squared). The general idea is that YOU are the Mass, and the faster you can move your "mass" through technique, the more kinetic energy you create to put into use. The makiwara board gives you an immediate physical and audio feedback at the same time to let you know how you are doing. It tells you other important things about your technique quality as well.

If you are not making a proper fist when punching, you quickly feel it. If you are doing front snap-kicks and not curling your toes back, you'll know right away. If you are not mentally focused on hitting the center of the pad, you may miss completely and lurch forwards, feeling really dumb. Or, you may peel the skin off of your limbs, hitting or skimming along the edge of the actual board. You may need a bandage. That can get messy.

Ideally, we use the makiwara to create *ikken hissatsu* type techniques, that have the ability to stop an opponent dead in their tracks. We begin with the driving force that a particular technique is designed to have, we do it with the highest velocity we can muster, and we slam into the dead center of the makiwara pad with "kime"(focus). With this *kime*, the object is to lock all the muscle groups together at the instant of contact. By locking your body weight together, you greatly increase the mass behind your technique. Instead of punching with just the weight of your arm, or kicking with only your foot, you are using the mass of you entire body. Driving forces are created from different body use, like moving forward, hip rotation, body vibration, etc. But the principle and energy transfer are nearly the same. In doing so correctly, the kinetic energy you've created is transferred directly into the point of contact, away from you into the target. If you have weak points at this particular instant in your body, for example: if your heels are up, if your fist is loose, if you are not anchored to the ground in a good stance, thne you absorb the energy coming back (Newton's Laws) and nullify your own efforts. If successful, on the other hand, all the kinetic energy you create goes outward into your intended target as a destructive shock wave.

But the beauty of the makiwara, I think, is that if you do everything correctly as you intended, it answers back with a successful "Whack!" You can spend hours of satisfied training with you punching post. It becomes a personal friend almost. It always gives you honest feedback.

If you treat your karate as Budo, it will be very useful to you when you need it. If you treat your karate as a past-time, you deceive yourself at its dependability in self-defense. Budo techniques were originally designed for use in unforgiving combat. For the most part, what we have now, survived an evolution of natural selection. Techniques that may have looked good but did not work, died out with their proponents. If techniques worked and kept one alive, they would be passed on. Nowadays, we have a tremendous amount of scientific knowledge in force production, correct technique performance, physiology, anatomy, kinesiology, and karate body dynamics, and more.

The makiwara is great preparation for technique use because it is what it is. It prepares one for hitting an attacker that is made of sinew and bone and probably wearing clothing or body armor. Much of hard core makiwara and board breaking traditions, we have been told in the literature, came from peasants needing to break through bamboo armor with their bare hands, to crush bones in ruthless warriors as they defended their lives and families.

If you are used to punching a makiwara for example, impacting bone on an attacker is an event your empty-handed technique is better prepared for. If you only train on bags with your hands padded to the hilt, you will surely have strong technique, but in bare-fisted fighting, your own fists and feet may self-destruct on impact. Mentioned earlier, Isaac Newton's laws of physics say that for every action there is an opposite and equal reaction. The force that travels outward through your fist must come simultaneously back. Training will help us send it outward into the intended target without our own body parts absorbing much force; self-destructing under shock wave we have created.

So, you face the makiwara, the punching post, in an anchored stance; cracked, bloodied, calloused knuckles punching. One, two, ten, a hundred! It hammers undaunted determination into the human spirit— energy, power, thought, all merge into a moment of *kime* with the punching post.

You soon realize ironically, that the more you relax at the beginning and throughout most of your punch, the faster the technique is, and the more kinetic energy and impact force is created and transferred in that last instant, into your imaginary opponent — the makiwara.

But as makiwara becomes your friend, it's hard to walk past it without the urge to hit it. It begs you to. "Crack!" Physical feedback is in the shock wave felt on impact with the sound of a small clap of thunder as force is cleanly delivered. If not, you know by the sound and the feel. All those things you learn suddenly come together for real, there is very little "fudge factor." You'll know the truth of your technique, good or bad, instantly.

Furthermore, your punching post fosters tenacity, correct timing and tension, expansion and contraction, breathing, and strengthens the determined, controlled mind set. It is the "anvil" that hammers the human spirit and karate technique into one. Your goal of the makiwara is *"ikken hissatsu,"* killing with one technique. If you are attacked by multiple attackers you are not fighting 10 rounds, you have a great need to eliminate one attacker with the lethal force in one technique. Time is not a luxury.

I asked Hirokazu Kanazawa Sensei once, how often, or how many punches we should practice on the makiwara each day. He said thoughtfully, "When you are young and learning, your body is stronger, but techniques haven't fully developed yet, so you can do hundreds. But when you get older and your techniques are stronger, but your body is more in risk of damage, 30-40 is plenty." Seemed like a "catch 22" in a good way, I think. I was in the younger category at that time when he told me, and my spirit is still strong and determined. But sometimes I confess, my mind wants to make bills that my body can't always pay. But I still love my makiwaras!

Each time we wind up and punch the makiwara, we are pulling the trigger on our best effort, and with a big kiai, we fuel our punch with our fighting spirit. Along with breathing, natural relaxation, the synchronized firing of muscle groups producing powerful driving forces, and trying to perfect kime through our target, we happily hammer away. Over five decades of karate, it brings me joy to see many of my students, now seasoned karateka who are now excellent instructors on their own, as they post pictures of themselves training on their own makiwaras. Summer and winter in heat and snow, indoors and out, it thrills me to see their joy in using their makiwara. It certainly forges our traditional karate spirit.

CHAPTER 25

Mountain Climbed: First Things First

BEFORE MAKING A DEVASTATING PUNCH, we must first learn to make a proper fist. Tight fingers turn our bare hand into a rock. Loose fingers can snap like twigs. In karate, there are stages of learning and development of the mind and body. All people progress at different rates according to their abilities and aptitudes.

Gyo is an introductory stage in traditional martial art training where virtually everything is new. *Dojo* etiquette and fundamentals are introduced. Brand new paradigms are formed which differentiate the *dojo*, a place for serious concentrated karate study, from the noise and distractions of ordinary life. This is a culture shock that departs considerably from the beginner's preconceived notions. For those spoiled by instant gratification, martial arts skill development may seem unbearable. Many would-be "warriors" don't last the first month.

But we all have to begin somewhere. This is an awkward stage as students try to copy the instructor's actions. Higher expectations of self-discipline and conduct are introduced as the beginner scrambles to cope with new challenges. It is a time of self-realization. Formerly perceived personal limits are pleasantly surpassed. Students may for the first time discover the true meaning of practicing one thing endlessly, until halted at the threshold of exhaustion. In traditional *dojos*, debates with the instructor are rare. The secret to success at this stage, building critical foundations, is listening to, copying the sensei, with relentless repetition and practice of punches, kicks, blocks and stances. Body tissues are broken down and rebuilt, renewed. Through devoted daily practice in and out of the *dojo*, techniques are ingrained. Gichin Funakoshi stressed that skill development is cumulative, and even minutes a day are valuable. From basic to advanced, karate is learned layer by layer, like floors in building a skyscraper. A strong foundation of skills and attitudes from this beginning stage is critical.

The fitness "dabbler" may experience novelty and exercise, but only the serious karate student will enjoy profound positive benefits. The attrition rate of beginners can be high. Karate is hard work. In fitness gyms people can read or watch TV while working out: not possible in the dojo.

Karate forces people into examining and confronting their own strengths and weaknesses. This may be the first time this process is a purposely welcome challenge! The vast majority of people quit karate before progressing through *gyo*. Their preconceptions of an easily won black belt status give way to the realization that karate skill results from endless hours of sweat on the *dojo* floor. With curiosity satisfied, an over-inflated ego threatened, or an aversion to just plain hard work, the insincere soon dropout. High spirited students catapult from their comfort zones and forge ahead. The nuts and bolts of hand and foot techniques, stances, body dynamics, breathing, mental skills, etiquette, ethics and vocabulary, are introduced and practiced with progressive intensity.

This is a culture shock for the person who walks in off the street, but it is the absolute prerequisite to all levels of skill. These rudimentary skills are reinforced in all higher levels of training. Through persistence, this skill "core" becomes internalized. Mental and physical patterns of response become reflexive through time. During prearranged sparring or application drills, techniques work well. But in these early stages, when speed is enthusiastically increased, technique quality degenerates. While many techniques seem easy, they are far from being dependable against high-spirited attackers. All astonishing personal triumphs, and defeats withstanding, this is just the beginning for higher karate stages. Every mountain climbed starts at the base.

CHAPTER 26

Deadly Force and Quality Human Beings:

Or, Speak Softly and…

IN OUR CLASSES, we formally bow in and out of class. It's not only a demonstration of respect, but this purposeful pause mentally puts everyone on "the same page." Normal daily distractions are blocked out to focus on our lessons. When kneeling, *"seiza"* position, we recite Funakoshi's *Dojo Kun* in Japanese and then in English.

Our *Dojo* "codes of behavior" can be roughly traced back to the mid-1700s to "Tode" Sakugawa in Okinawa. Sakugawa responsible for Shuri castle security was noted for instructing *"Bushi Matsumura"* (who later became chief of security for 50 years.) By day, they performed administrative and diplomatic duties with ceremony and decorum; by night, trained to protect the royal family by killing with their bare hands. Character development and powerful effective karate were unified.

I could go down a long list of respected karate founders, masters, and legends that we all admire, that all stress the importance of nonviolence and positive character development that are only outlined in the Dojo Codes of traditional karate styles.

Karate-do can develop higher quality human beings. Character compliments devastating technique. Or, as America's President Theodore Roosevelt often said, **"Speak softly and carry a big stick!"**

It's not enough to robotically recite a code of conduct. It has to be explained in terms that students of all ages, maturity levels, living environments, social context, etc. can understand. You make have ten-year-olds or sixty-year-olds in a basic class. These ideals have to be presented so all understand. Here are some practical suggestions for presenting them in a short context that is easily understood but of course instructors can elaborate as much as they wish depending on the class demographics, ages, etc.

Let's take a quick look:

Striving for the perfection of character!

Simply put; this is a process of trying to be a better person than you were the day before. Adults get it. With children, you can teach this in terms of being a "good citizen," and showing respectful behavior to others. Teach them never to bully, but to try to help others. Change words to fit your audience, but the idea is the same: improving character is everyday training, just like technique.

Follow a path of sincerity and honesty!

This is a directive to be sincere and honest while dealing with others. It develops and demonstrates integrity. The more we practice sincerity and honesty, we make more good choices. New challenges come. Principally driven with sincerity and honesty, you gain respect, credibility, and inner strength.

Foster the spirit of effort!

Expect enthusiasm to be highly visible in the dojo! "Fostering the spirit" of enthusiasm and effort simply means that we should wake up each day, take a deep breath, and give it our best shot! Whether at school or work, Karate helps us to try hard to never, ever give up! Enthusiasm is contagious! You'll quickly see it energize your students!

Being polite, respectful, and courteous

People sometimes think there's a contradiction in teaching students to punch and kick people, while telling them to be courteous and humble at the same time. Contradictory? Not in authentic karate. It's especially critical in teaching kids to demonstrate that proper etiquette, courtesy, and the like, is a strength! The more courteous and respectful you are in and out of the dojo, the more people will reciprocate similar behaviors to you: more harmony brought into our world.

Refrain from impetuousness!

Simplified sometimes to, "Control your temper," if you have no self-control, you do not belong in karate. It's also a weakness easily capitalized on by skilled opponents. If you tend to be impetuous, you jump to conclusions and make blunders. Ignoring this ideal can dishonor you, your martial art, and create legal issues. Karate is a deadly force not to be misused. After teaching karate in high schools and community centers for decades, administrations and the parents welcome high-spirited, rough and tumble activities. Violent, undisciplined behavior is detrimental and destroys the credibility of karate clubs, students, and instructors.

Just as we train students to ward off physical attacks, we have to train them to ward off psychological, verbal attacks and the like. Karate done correctly is wielding deadly force. Being a responsible karateka is trying to be a better person and understanding that non-violence and strong integrity is demanded by karate in its truest sense. In practical terms, remember that each use of karate in self-defense will probably have lawyers close behind. Serious study of *Dojo Kun* helps us face stressful challenges. We can learn integrity with calm determination in today's hectic world — be the eye of the hurricane.

CHAPTER 27

Of Shrikes and Men: Getting the Sharper Edge

I CONFESS. Often the pace of watching MLB baseball on TV might cause me to nap, or to peruse karate images and videos as my family cheers on their team. My wife grew up in Chicagoland and is a huge Chicago Cub fan. So, I am diplomatic and careful…just saying. I do watch batting and throwing to analyze rotation, stances, pendulum motions, or anything that looks like a possible karate power generating component that they might be using. Professional level baseball, golf, tennis, boxing, or anything I can learn from, is good. No matter the muscular activity, much boils down to power (force) = mass (muscle groups and body weight, etc.) multiplied by velocity (speed). Most physical/sports activities use the same principles as in karate for creating body kinetic energy. Warriors were researching long before modern team sports were invented.

Most of us look everywhere, looking for anything to learn from, to make our karate better. Karate people were cross-training before it was a term. At the same time, we use karate to improve many physical and mental areas of our lives. Many of my karate friends play golf, using hip rotations to swing with mental focus. I enjoy archery and precision firearm shooting for what I call, "Shooting Zen."

I watched the MLB, All-Star Game Home Run Derby. I enjoy watching professional and Olympic level skills. I enjoyed just watching them blast homeruns; hoping I could punch that hard, of course. I watched their techniques, differing stances, rotations, their eyes perceiving the incoming ball to precisely connect with and crack! Motion transferred to energy and transferred to the soaring ball.

Then, oddly below, a scrolling text announced a controversy. There were more home runs lately because the baseball manufacturers were stitching the baseballs tighter. Scandalous! Fans were thinking about statistics, how the balls used to be sewn, and so forth. Not me. My mind went to punching! Stitching balls tighter was like making a tighter fist, that very last instant, efficiently transferring kinetic energy into impact in a knockout punch. The batter rotates, quickly swinging from his solid stance, making bat contact into the new and tighter ball. Energy transferred more efficiently, and the ball goes further. No mystery there: sound parallel karate scientific principles.

If you train with a makiwara, this is something the makiwara "teaches" you quickly. Starting relaxed, doing a high-speed punch, tensing your fist tightly before impact, and whack! If you don't tense your fist properly, the cracking sound you hear may be a broken hand. Or, it may have the muffled sound (of a bean bag) as your hand absorbs, rather than transfers that energy. Check out the Facebook group, "Fans of Makiwara Training" and peruse folks experimenting with makiwaras of all sorts. The effects are clear.

In karate, as other traditional martial arts with rich evolving histories, practitioners studied anything they thought would give a sharper edge to their art. Much was learned from combat as the ultimate source of knowledge in tactics and strategies. As nowadays, the bottom line is personal preparedness and skill development for all eventualities.

Martial arts legends were always critical observers seeking to apply anything to give them an advantage. Life and death were real consequences. I'm fond of reading about Musashi, from his own hand in *The Book of Five Rings* and other biographical accounts of his training, his fighting adventures, and his pilgrimages into the mountains. While browsing through one of my fine art books, the artist name Miyamoto Musashi popped out at me! An ink drawing of a little bird, a Shrike, sitting on a thin twig, was standing over smooth still water. The Shrike was famous for sitting motionless, patiently, waiting for its victim. Its meal would sense no tell-tale motion above until it was too late. Musashi appreciated greatly to express it in his art. The Shrike is known as "Butcher bird." We can learn from all that is around us.

CHAPTER 28

Keep it Real

WHILE THUMBING THROUGH *Karate-do: My Way of Life*, by Gichin Funakoshi, a few lines he simply called "Important Points" caught my eye. (In many ways, in his literature, Funakoshi was a master of the understatement.) "Strict observance" of these, he warns, is "absolutely essential" to understanding the "true nature of karate." (Not a soft-sell, but to the point!) Easily a long chapter in any book, I can really only scratch the surface here. I always enjoy reading what is "proper training," in the words and context of Funakoshi and his peers, across all traditional Karate styles. It's intriguing to see their perspectives on realistically applying karate into everyday lives. Clearly, they did it to obsession until it became a natural part of them. From an unforgiving era when there were no cell phones to call for help, and no referees to yell "stop", they really force us to re-examine our methods and mind sets, to examine the correctness of our paradigms… reality check.

Funakoshi says, "you must be deadly serious in training" and that "your opponent must always be present in your mind, whether you sit, stand, or walk." For the eventuality of using karate in real life, Funakoshi is adamant that; if "one blow decides everything," he doesn't mean a round, or a match... he means EVERYTHING.

In my favorite clinics with Master Osamu Ozawa (a direct student of Funakoshi), he often sternly insisted, "Always show your intent to hit your partner when you attack!" He said this gives the right "spirit" or feeling that Funakoshi Sensei intended. And whenever partner training, a good aggressive attack is needed to make better defense training. FBI violent crime statistics have shown that the average attack or fight confrontation lasts about three to five seconds. While at first beginners need to be taught slowly so that they can learn and develop skills, after they start using them in partner training and gain proficiency and confidence, the intensity must be ratcheted up. Especially at advanced levels, showing each other the "intention of hitting" with full-speed and high-spirited shouting makes better realism. Actual use during a very real assault cannot be predicted, but at least martial art skill sets can have been developed to increase survivability. In class, instructors must control contact and monitor safety, but I love to encourage rowdy enthusiastic attacks and counter attacking; to be so loud and fierce, that neither participant is sure that their training partner is not trying to "bury punches to the elbow!" Once the exchange begins, it should be as realistic as possible. I encourage students that while we are following karate attack-training karate etiquette, that they should block, parry, and counter as if their partner will hit them. And besides, I remind them, your partner might slip in sweat and smash their nose. So, they MUST treat every attack as real! If attacks are held back, then the blocker may wrongly assume that they have learned a proper defense. Partners in full speed training must have their internal controls turned on, but if they are not showing an outward strong, high spirited intent, then then are doing their partner a very real disservice. Incorrect training only produces incorrect results. After repetitive quality practice, however, then students learn to be more capable in violent, more explosive environments. As Funakoshi said, "one blow could decide everything." It all comes back to training.

With the evolution of karate competition, experiences among highly trained competitors can be productive for many. Indeed, with karate in the Olympics, high levels of karate skills will be demonstrated by people who have dedicated their lives to karate. Karate competition will be showcased, and the world will be watching. Tournaments are excellent arenas to test full speed skills against other completely unknown opponents in a limited amount of time. Those experiences can burn a healthy imprint in the minds of competitors and observers alike. Many of the instructors highlighted in this book have learned much in international competitions that they now freely share with young students. Experience is a great teacher.

Admittedly, I lean toward karate-do as applied to a lifestyle that benefits everyone: fit athletes, average people of all ages, a wide spectrum of physical abilities, folks from all walks of life, who can benefit from its many benefits. Lessons from Funakoshi and others clearly portray karate-do as a character strengthening, physical and mental, daily lifestyle. It is at best, not merely a passing hobby like the newest fitness fads we see every day. It is incredibly more. Modern life is inherently dangerous and under a very thin veil of civility;

authentic karate training in our world should still be taken quite seriously. Understanding "its true nature," is just as valuable now as any time in history, as solutions to coping with the crazy world around us.

Even the remote possibility that Funakoshi's "one blow" might "decide everything," should give pause for thought. Maybe a very chilling thought. You may only have time for one effective technique; and no time to get fancy. That in mind, the *makiwara* can be your new best friend too. With the possibility of an attack coming from up close and personal, it is particularly helpful in developing the sudden, high impact shock waves, through short distances, that you might need. It instantly gives you impressive feedback on how much kinetic energy your technique can deliver. Because of its design and purpose, the makiwara shows you if your techniques are being performed correctly. If your fist is not correct, or your trajectory is not accurate, you know immediately, sometimes painfully. In contrast it gives sound feedback, and a correct "feel," if you are relaxing and tensing, expanding contracting, mentally focused or distracted, and more. The makiwara is a wonderfully, invaluable traditional training aide. Punching bags are great for their many purposes; but attackers are made of bone, cartilage, sinew, and your empty hands are not normally taped up in boxing gloves. There is a difference.

But then, karate is an emptyhanded fighting method.

Funakoshi saying that the opponent "must always be present in your mind, whether you sit, stand, or walk," brings to mind my own childhood, when my father was a police officer.

It was amusing for me as a child (almost a game) going into a restaurant, to argue over whose chair would get the best view of the door: your back to a wall, not windows - extra credit. Funakoshi saying that an opponent must always be in your mind, addresses many levels of awareness. This is not paranoia, just a habit of reasonable caution and knowing what is around you. With a heightened sense of awareness, you might avoid being surprised or in a position to where life is needlessly in danger. To define types of awareness to students, of course we are on the watch for "bad guys," but being aware of our surroundings also helps us, for example, to not walk out in front of a truck!

Situational awareness is critical in everyday life; even just walking or driving, for instance. Surveys show that prison inmates, convicted of assaults, rapes, murders, and the like, prefer victims who are simply not paying attention to what is going on around them. This is not rocket science, but it's certainly a wake-up call. Walking around with our headphones in our ears and our nose into our cell phones may be cause for concern.

And then there's the so-called "21-foot rule." All law enforcement officers are aware of it. It's a rough distance that, even against armed officers or concealed weapon carrying citizens, for example, bad guys can charge in with a bladed weapon, striking or slashing, before a side-arm can be deployed. An FBI instructor told me that charging in on that distance is a fun game in the prison yard for inmates. He said one day he watched as they took turns charging in on each other, pretending that one was a policeman with a side arm, and that they would run in pretending to stab them. The agent said they were having great fun – and training? Even carrying a firearm, your empty hand skill sets are always a valuable first line of defense.

CHAPTER 29

Nothing Stays the Same

THROUGH THE TREMENDOUS STRUGGLE and hard work by thousands of credible like-minded people, martial arts of many sorts are in the mainstream of our society; in the Olympics, Pam Am Games, all sorts of TV, movies, and the like. Karate is woven throughout society. Traditional karate-do as intended by the founders with traditional values and long-term training goals of lifestyle development of the mind and body of ordinary people is not often portrayed. The international acceptance nowadays makes it somewhat easier to find a dojo to your liking that fits your personal needs.

There is a joke that marketing folks can't get rich from traditional karate students because all they feel they need is an occasional new plain uniform and a mouth guard. In over five decades of training in traditional karate, I have been amused at the evolution of the variety of "stuff" that is marketed for martial arts types, organizations, and activities. Okay, most associations proudly display their club logo on patches, pins, banners and more. From the traditional point of view, for the most part, with no offense intended, the multicolored, star spangled, embroidered neon glittered uniforms are, well, "the other guys."

Entering the traditional dojo for the purpose of training in the martial way is not at all like merely stepping into a new exercise room. It is often entering an entirely new way of thinking. Just be brave. Go for it! If you do you can experience extraordinary positive personal growth and self-respect. Take family members as well! Progress is the realization of your new accomplishments. Even small improvements are BIG.

In karate-do there must be only the unwavering search for improvement, for knowledge, ethics, health, fitness, truth, and for conquering our weaknesses for meeting the challenges ahead, that life is guaranteed to throw upon us. We also learn the important life skill of always trying to raise our own bar.

All progress is good progress.

The strengths we accumulate through reinforcement of our karate principles are far more important than to be used in just self-defense and sport karate. Granted if you only have to use karate to save your life just once, of course all your hard work is worth it!

But there is much more. We need to build inner strength for the long haul.

The karate lifestyle, in *Budo*, is a reservoir we can draw on for inner strength. Through serious training our thought patterns change to a more positive outlook, that is much less easily shaken by adversity. In fact, we practice facing challenges that seem impossible to overcome each and every practice on purpose! Real life and death challenges can be incredibly humbling. They may come as complete surprises. Tragedies out of our control can suddenly attack us and our loved ones like accidents, illness, and the like. In seconds, lives can be changed forever. And even if we live a charmed life, as we age, our own bodies will turn against us! Seek to be strong because life is unforgiving for the weak and unsuspecting.

Moving Forward Boldly

If you only have to use karate to save your life just once...

Once you enter and stay in a quality dojo, change will be for the best, and you will never be the same. Even if you train only two or three times a week you will notice improvement in the first month that will make you feel great mentally and physically. Your body will begin adjusting, muscles will wake up and grow. As your cardiovascular system improves, your thinking will improve, and a new positive outlook will emerge. It gets easier and the good feelings snowball. If you can train three times or six times a week, great! But If you train hard for an hour, your muscular skeletal systems grow and increase your body's metabolism for at least two days after. If you use muscles hard and stress them, they rebuild in forty-eight hours stronger. So, in addition to just the physiological effects, you are also learning to use your newly awakened muscle groups performing karate techniques. You are not just improving fitness but doing so with new and valuable skills.

> **"If you are not moving forward, you are moving backward. Nothing stays the same."**
> -- GICHIN FUNAKOSHI

In the literature, karate training often was conducted in the yard of the sensei, often in the dark, often in secret, always in fierce determination, and always in humility. The location of the training was of little importance. In karate, star-spangled gyms with mega-marketing are not necessary. All that is needed is an instructor, a student, training and learning, and the correct mindset: the karate spirit. Training in karate-do can be a lifetime enjoyable endeavor; not for tournaments, not for warrior ninja television shows, but just for the training's sake; as a lifestyle. It is not merely a flip hobby that you are doing, eventually it may become who you are.

What Degree Are You?

One day after class, a wide-eyed parent emerged from the crowd of spectators to pick up his son. He pointed at my belt and said, "Is that a black belt?" It was a worn-out and ragged looking belt, more white than black, threads hanging in disarray, the once golden embroidered kanji barely recognizable.

A little embarrassed, I replied, "Yes Sir."

Seemingly amazed he prodded loudly, "Well, just what degree are you?"

I looked down at my tattered, ragged, gray and white speckled, shredded belt, shrugged my shoulders and said, "Just old, I guess."

Karate-Do can simply become who you are.

Epilogue

KARATE TAUGHT in the comprehensive traditional karate manner has a tremendous empowering result for us all! It has probably more value today than ever, especially dealing with the complex bombardment of social media, marketing, political media manipulation, stress in the work environment and the violence that is still present in today's society. Physically, karate-do is an ideal path to a healthy lifestyle that is imbedded within the correct development of karate technical skill sets; that after hundreds of years, are still as valuable in unarmed, empty-hand combat as ever. Mentally, the manner of proper disciplined training of the conscious and subconscious mind, is a critical component in karate because it directs the intensity and the successful implementation of all physical activity. In addition, the mental dispositions successfully learned and valued in authentic traditional karate styles promote nonviolence, stress management, and harmony. Clearly, comprehensive karate training gives participants mental and physical power to be a better human being and to contribute positively to civilization. Not to sound skeptical, but civilization is fragile and depends on the even keel of many factors. It can be a thin veil. When the beasts of human greed, aggression, and insensitivity rear their ugly head, the need for people of strong, positive, non-violent character, with the skills of *budo* are precious. That kind of brings us full circle to the original reasons for the fundamental human need to survive, that stimulated karate evolution from in the beginning.

I've shown that empowering, comprehensive karate training is very multifaceted. There is the calm, deliberately common-sense, self-disciplined conduct outlined in the *Dojo Kun* of Master Funakoshi. And, in contrast, there is the ever-aware, split-second, explosive and trained subconscious directed appropriate reactions to danger that would nullify even a ferocious animal. There is the "Peaceful Spirit" that the likes of Funakoshi, Nakayama, Ozawa, Kawawada, and their peers stressed was the essence, and indeed, a major requirement for True Karate. And there is Musashi's "Void"; the highest stage where so much accumulated training is internalized the expert in *budo* can react appropriately, without any prior indication of danger, at any time or place. What all have in common is dedicated and proper disciplined technical training of the body with the conscious and subconscious mind, coupled with the internalization of it all. It should be noted that most of our legendary karate heroes lived a healthier lifestyle than most of their non-training contemporaries of the day. Though knowledge of their bad habits does not go unaccounted for. Many of them lived far beyond the typical life spans of the day. With the attention to healthier lifestyles, the activities inherent in karate, and with the knowledge of health and nutrition that has grown exponentially nowadays, we are potentially far better off. As life spans get longer, the importance of keeping the body active and the mind engaged is the perfect floorplan for us. As youth and the feeling of invincibility, social pressures and temptations, and lack of positive influences for young people, the benefits of karate for them increase; and the bars of good karate instructors are raised.

Positive high-spiritedness is not unique to karate, which validates its importance even more. Every military branch — army, navy, air force, marines and so on — instill exponential levels of enthusiasm, high-spirited patriotism and comradeship.

All athletic teams, professional and amateur, nurture spirit training because they know that if equally matched teams collide on the field, the one with the strongest individual and combined mental strength and enthusiasm will prevail. This brings us full circle to the contention that if two adversaries in martial arts are evenly matched, the mentally stronger will win. If excellent qualities of performance are the required norm, then spirit training is essential.

Through excellent long-term karate training, new patterns of thinking and behavior begin. But just as Funakoshi is quoted, "Karate is like boiling water. Without continuous heat, it will soon become cold." So it is, that the physical and mental benefits that empower us, require regular practice. The good news is that if something is really good, and you get away from it for a while, it's still good when you return. I've experienced several major life-threatening setbacks, yet doing any kind of karate training at all, that I have been able to do, makes me feel that I have a little more power to come back to "normal," regain my strength and determination; like Stan Schmidt using a rock as a makiwara in his hospital bed to reclaim his own karate strength of spirit.

A clearly focused mind is the best conduit to direct high-spirited energy resulting in quite remarkable skill sets. Compare that someone who comes to karate practice just for the exercise; satisfying curiosity, wanting to lose a couple pounds, and maybe to get "that burn" that signals a short-term stimulant to muscle growth. You will instantly observe the clear contrast with the skilled *karateka* who trains with purpose and with clear-minded focus. The difference will be remarkable --- no contest. And if these two hypothetical examples are attacked violently, the results will differ considerably. Our karate as-a-hobby person might, squeak by with limited physical strength and some luck. Our serious karate student who trains both mental and physical skill sets will be a much more competent and dangerous person for an attacker to deal with.

You can take back control. Empowered with comprehensive karate training in the topics and abilities presented here, other aspects of your life are affected and improved: daily living, as it is for all of us, is an up-hill struggle. If you do not act, you will be acted upon. That's just life. We cannot merely occupy space and use up oxygen. Proactive effort is a must. "If you are not moving forward, you are moving backward. Nothing stays the same." You can eventually become a victim of your own complacent behavior. But if you diligently train your body, your mind, and your spirit, you will be prepared for all sorts of unexpected challenges.

> **"If you are not moving forward, then you are moving backward. NOTHING stays the same."**

Karate training perspectives are healthy. Obstacles become challenges, and your attitude takes on a positive and confident disposition. Some people see the mountain as a disappointing insurmountable blockade. Others, with a positive attitude and faith, see a beautiful landscape and a fresh challenge to stimulate and invigorate; a place to feel really alive. Mountain climbers are famous for a never-give-up, enthusiastic spirit. The often-exemplary reply to the question posed to them, like; "Why do you want to climb a mountain?" is usually answered by the average climber as simply; "Because, it is there."

Sadly, we've all seen people on ego trips that just don't belong in karate. Karate training is not about self-indulgence. We must make self-reassessments, honest judgments about our own progress, and then to begin self-motivated actions toward improvement. This is a habit we learn in training. It is an exercise in facing yourself honestly, and it's certainly not easy. Dojos do not have mirrors, so we can admire our good looks (sorry). The mirrors are all about blunt honesty in your self-assessments. They neither flatter nor degrade you. They just show you what is. In most dojos you'll hear comments of self-scorn when advanced students see themselves in the mirror. "Darn, it felt a lot better than it looks!"

If we are motivated to "raise our own bar," raise our own standards, heighten self-expectations, increase your achievement; we will become better and better each day.

According to Master Nakayama, at the highest stage of training; after years of training the body, mind, and spirit, in all aspects of karate, techniques are applied without the need for thought. For you and me, that means training until it is impossible to tell where our technique begins and ends. Does it start with an aggressive twitch from an opponent toward us, or does it start with the instant we recognize the smallest impression that a threat may be pending? Sometimes the techniques used are not known until conflict is over. I've known many excellent competitors who in *kumite*, did not know that they even attacked until they were stopped by the referee. I've met *karateka* who were victims of foul play and who reacted without thinking to overpower an assailant. They react in a rather calm, yet explosive high-spirited fashion without thinking; all their actions were a blur to them. Like a car accident, the shaking, the heavy sigh, and adrenalin dump came afterward. This is critical in self-defense because the average attack scenario lasts only a couple seconds; a couple of heartbeats determine the outcome. Long term karate training glues the initial recognition of danger to the actions taken more seamlessly.

Knowing only techniques without proper mental preparation allows openings for fear and self-doubt to creep to cloud the mind and to temporarily paralyze and slow down muscular actions; the techniques needed. Becoming paralyzed with fear is more than an expression. It is a life-threatening reality. Training to "the highest stage," where mind and body action are flawlessly fused, breeds successful survival skill.

Instead of the mindset of becoming the victim, we can become the consequence.

If training the mind and body to their highest potential is real, then we should find it to be a common denominator in other extreme life-threatening situations; and we do. Look no further than all first responders trained in your own community. I was recently in a hospital intensive care department, quietly healing from surgery, in the middle of the night, when a "code blue" suddenly rang out. Someone had collapsed in the ICU room next to me!

The place exploded into action with nurses and doctors running from all directions to the victim. They converged in teams to revive my neighbor. Individuals with specialty skills reacted instantly from whatever they were doing and converged to become a lifesaving team. It was a superb level of internalized skill converging as one to save a life. Likewise, first-responders fire fighters, police, and ambulance personal with years of experience have trained to a level where reactions are deeply trained. These responders deal with life and death as a daily norm to help us all.

Karate-do EMPOWERS you to succeed as becomes part of your lifestyle. Done well it is comprehensive "life training." As karate training becomes an expression of who you are, it affects positive outcome from your attitudes and behavior, thought processes, attitudes, and actions; according to the high standards of *Budo*, the martial way.

Of course, as we age, scar tissue stiffens in the cold, joints grind, and the soft tissues don't stretch like they used to. However, comprehensive karate training becomes even more necessary, reviving our health, and coming to our aid with holistic benefits. After all, getting older isn't for wimps!

One of our frequent training "inconveniences" to rise above is pain. Pain can be a friend or foe. Pain can be a helpful indicator of injury or an annoying daily visitor. In the absence of purpose and motivation, enthusiasm and goals, any amount of pain can slap us down. It can be disabling, even in small doses. Encouragement lies with an empowered karate disposition, exhilaration, determination, a sense of purpose and more joy; pain does not have to have complete power over us. Accompanied by enthusiastic goals it is diminished and with a superior motivation it can become a strong stimulant for necessary and positive changes you need to make in your life.

Awareness is one of the most critical mental skills anyone can learn for everyday use. Awareness is a mental state or skill that must be active when all others are on hold. There are varying degrees and types of awareness. But being aware of what is going on around you as you move through your daily life, walking in the city, driving, cycling, enjoying recreation is a no-brainer. One concept is *Tsuki no Kokoro*, or "mind like the moon". As the moon's rays on a moonlit night softly glow on everything below it on earth, so should your attention be broad and flowing out around you, so you miss nothing within range of your senses. You perceive all both small and large, obvious and obscured, just as the rays of the moon blanket the earth.

Mizu no Kokoro, or "mind like water" is a mental state that allows your mind to be clear and calm like the glassy surface of a calm lake. It is effectively a mirror that calmly reflects accurately all that you might see as you gaze upon its surface.

Drawing from this analogy, if our mind is filled with thoughts of fear, lack of confidence, and anxiety, and "what ifs," then we cannot accurately perceive the threat and react correctly. If confronted with danger and your mind is calm and clear, we will more accurately perceive the threat and react correctly to deal with it.

Combining *Mizu no Kokoro* and *Tsuki no Kokoro* in our training, the result is that have the power to more correctly see a threat and correctly react to it as needed.

Karate training may be just the ticket to cope with your high stressed lifestyle to bring it all into proper focus and keep you mentally and physically healthy. Or when the lights go out, the laws of civility break down, and the beasts truly get hungry, dedicated karate spirit and training can improve survivability. Make no mistake; karate is a warrior art, *budo*, that even to present day, forges the individual into a peaceful, stronger, more aware, more capable and productive and happier human being.

Bibliography

Brewer, R.L.B., ME, (2018). Karate Insights: Lessons for Life. Los Angeles, California. United States: Empire Books.

Clayton, B. D., Ph.D. (2004). Shotokan's Secret. United States: Ohara Publications, Inc.

Draeger, D. F. (1973). Classical Budo Volume Two. New York, New York: Weatherhill, Incorporated.

Enoeda, K., & Mack, C. J. (1974). Shotokan Karate: Free Fighting Techniques. London: Paul H. Crompton Ltd.

Funakoshi, G. (1973). Karate-Do Kyohan: The Master Text (T. Ohshima, Trans.). Tokyo, Japan: Kodansha International, Ltd.

Funakoshi, G. (1975). Karate-Do: My Way of Life. Tokyo, Japan: Kodansha International.

Funakoshi, G. (1988). Karate-Do Nyumon. Tokyo: Kodansha International Ltd.

Funakoshi, G. (1994). To-Te Jitsu (S. Ichida, Trans.). Hamilton, Ontario, Canada: Masters Publication. (Original work published 1922)

Funakoshi, G. (2003). The Twenty Guiding Principles of Karate. Tokyo, Japan: Kodansha International.

Funakoshi, G. (2005). Karate Do Kyohan (H. Suzuki-Johnston, Trans.). San Diego, CA: Neptune Publications.

Hassell, R. G. (1983). Conversations with the Master: Masatoshi Nakayama. St. Louis, MO: Focus Publications.

Hassell, R. G. (1984). Shotokan Karate: Its History and Evolution. St. Louis, MO: Focus Publications.

Hassell, R. G. (1989). The Karate Spirit. St. Louis, MO: Focus Publications.

Hassell, R. G. (1991). Karate Ideals. St. Louis, MO: Focus Publications.

Hassell, R. G. (1991). Karate Training Guide. St. Louis, MO: Focus Publications.

Hassell, R. G. (1993). Zen Pen and Sword: The Karate Experience. St. Louis, MO: Focus Publications.

Hassell, R. G., & Otis, E. (2000). The Complete Idiot's Guide to Karate (R. L. Brewer, Ed.). Indianapolis, Indiana: Alpha Books, Macmillan USA, Inc.

Kanazawa, H. (1982). Shotokan Karate International Kata (Volume 2). Japan: Author.

Kanazawa, H. (2004). Karate Fighting Techniques: The Complete Kumite. Tokyo, Japan: Kodansha International.

Musashi, M. (1982). A Book of Five Rings (V. Harris, Trans.). Woodstock, NY: The Overlook Press.

Nakayama, M. (1966). Dynamic Karate. Tokyo, Japan: Kodansha International Ltd.

Nakayama, M., & Draeger, D. F. (1963). Practical Karate 1. Tokyo, Japan: Tuttle Publishing.

Nakayama, M., & Draeger, D. F. (1964). Practical Karate 4: Defense Against Armed Assailants. Boston: Tuttle Publishing.

Nicol, C. W. (1975). Moving Zen. New York: Quill.

Nishiyama, H., & Brown, R. C. (1959). Karate: The Art of "Empty Hand" Fighting. Tokyo, Japan: Charles E. Tuttle Company, Incorporated.

Reilly, R. L. (1985). Complete Shotokan Karate. Boston: Charles E. Tuttle Company, Inc.

Schmidt, S. (1984). Spirit of the Empty Hand. St. Louis, MO: Focus Publications.

Schmidt, S. (1985). Recognition. St. Louis, MO: Focus Publications.

Schmidt, S. (1997). Meeting Myself: Beyond Spirit of the Empty Hand. St. Louis, MO: Focus Publications.

Sugiyama, S. (1984). 25 Shotokan Kata. United States: J. Toguri Mercantile Co.

Suzuki, S. (1970). Zen Mind, Beginner's Mind. New York, NY: Weatherhill, Inc.

Tokitsu, K. (n.d.). Miyamoto Musashi: His Life and Writings (S. C. Kohn, Trans.) Boston: Weatherhill.

Tzu, S. (1963). The Art of War (S. B. Griffith, Trans.). London: Oxford University Pre

Glossary of Instructors

AOKI, Isao: Isao Aoki Sensei was a student of Shoji Sensei in the JKA and was a former All Japan Champion. He had earned a reputation of visiting dojos all over and sparred with many of their best competitors just to improve his own skills. He then became an ISKF instructor and is listed in Kanazawa's Kumite Kyohan book. As many karate masters who have had seemingly impossible challengers, Aoki Sensei was in a car accident, and told he would never walk again. But later, he would be back doing karate. In the 1980s Aoki was Ted Quinn's instructor in Japan at the Yakota Air Base karate club. (Chapter 13) Some years ago, at an ASKA clinic taught by Sensei Randall Hassell, Ted Quinn met Sensei Sonny Kim and they struck up a wonderful conversation, and Sensei Kim shared with Quinn that his own instructor had trained with Isao Aoki in Japan as well. Small world! Aoki also trained Japanese police. One night he was dozing on a train just after teaching at the Yakota AB classes, a young punk was harassing people and grabbed his arm to wake him. Aoki side kicked him, and the bad guy staggered into the next car.

BAIN, Jason: Sensei Jason Bain started karate in 2003 in Western Illinois University under Sensei Ed Kuras. Then he moved to the Pekin Illinois and trained in the Central Illinois Shotokan Karate Association in the Mapleton and Pekin-area dojos where he earned his Shodan. As a Nidan, he has been assisting and teaching in the Central Illinois Shotokan Karate in the Peoria County FFA club and other Tazewell county dojos teaching youth and adults alike.

BREWER, Ben, MD: Ben Brewer is a physician who started karate training in 1981 in the Central Illinois Karate Association and Central Illinois Shotokan. In addition to his thriving medical practice and his karate activities, he is a published author in medical literature, and for several years, had a regular column in the *Wall Street Journal*. Brewer has taught karate at Illinois State University and assisted in the Illinois Wesleyan University accredited programs as well. Dr. Brewer currently trains and assists programs at the Central Illinois Shotokan Karate Association in Bloomington, Illinois. He is a 3rd Dan in the Central States Shotokan.

BUSHA, Michael: Michael Busha has been training since the early 1980s. He began karate training at the University of Michigan, and then traveled to Japan to train at both the Hoitsugan and the Honbu Dojos. He trained in the JKA Honbu Dojo and in the Hoitsugan, many of his most fond memories are training Masatoshi Nakayama and with Minoru Kawawada, who since Nakayama's passing, was appointed Chief Instructor of the Hoitsugan.

He is a Central States Shotokan 5th Dan, an ISKF 4th Dan, and a 3rd Dan in the JKA.

He is a CISKA Senior Instructor and is featured in the 2019 Central States Shotokan Seminars DVD (em3Video, Productions.) Michael and his wife Tomoko, also a 2nd Dan in Shotokan karate, have both been training in Central Illinois Shotokan Karate in the U.S. for over ten years together. Michael has been published in *Shotokan Karate Magazine* and has written the book, *Never Heel UP*, about his life and his training and experiences in Japan.

BUSHA, Tomoko: Sensei Tomoko Busha, was born in Japan and since marrying Michael Busha, now lives in the US. She trains regularly in their home dojo as well as trains, and is an Assistant Instructor, in The Central Illinois Shotokan Karate Association. Tomoko Sensei is a Shotokan Karate 2nd Dan and works for the Illinois Conservancy to conserve natural resources, land, and wildlife. Tomoko and Michael visit her parents in Japan as often as possible and hope to retire in Japan.

COOK, Dan: Dan has been training Karate since the age of 15 years old when he began under Sensei James Field at ISKF Santa Monica, California. Cook Sensei lived at the Hoitsugan for 9 years in the 1990s and on the Hoitsugan kata team that placed 3rd in JKA All-Tokyo Championships in 1996. Dan speaks fluent Japanese and lives and trains in Japan at the Hoitsugan where he assists Sensei Minoru Kawawada, the Chief Instructor of the Hoitsugan Dojo. Dan is a wonderful, warm and encouraging person with a great sense of humor who teaches English in Japanese Universities. Dan also has a Tokaido uniform and sales web site on-line in Japan that he manages. He is highly skilled in Shotokan karate-do and trains with some of the best karate instructors in Japan. He trains and assists in teaching visiting groups from dojos around the world who come to Japan to train in the Hoitsugan. Dan has been wonderful in assisting the author in hosting Kawawada Sensei's international trips to the Midwest, USA, and in fulfilling visit requests from instructors from many continents world-wide.

DALCHER, Josh: Josh Dalcher started karate in a small Boys and Girls Club program in Pekin, Central Illinois Shotokan Illinois and trained and competed all through high school and college. Trained with USA coach, Sensei Ed Kuras in the Western Illinois University Karate club. Following college, employed by Caterpillar, he moved to Denver and trains with Yaguchi Sensei's dojos with Mark Tarrant Sensei. His father Bob Dalcher is a brown belt still involved in karate-do, his family and firearm expertise. Josh Dalcher is a karateka who is also very active with his church and community.

DUKES, Matt: Sensei Matt Dukes is a 3rd Dan in Shotokan promoted by Sensei Randall Hassell in the ASKA and has practiced Shotokan for thirty years. Dukes worked for Illinois State University and Caterpillar in technology and web design. He is an instructor and highly skilled teaching all ages. He has been integral in spreading the word of traditional karate contributed greatly to many karate websites and Facebook pages allowing karate students to communicate worldwide. His wife Sarah is a brown belt known especially known for her kumite skills.

ERBE, David: Dave Erbe is an instructor who has been training for over thirty years and is a Nidan who teaches and assists in programs in the Central Illinois Shotokan, teaching youth and adults alike. He has been a huge inspiration to all instructors and students who know him, again like many karateka, using training to face life and death challenges, has fought his way back from a serious bout with cancer. He is now training and assisting in the dojo again and is even active in his motorcycle club organizing charity road rallies to help the less fortunate in his community. He is a true spirited karateka.

EVANS, Brian: Brian Evans started training in the Pekin High School Karate Club in the 1970s and competed on the high school competition team. He was an assistant instructor in the Pekin, Central Illinois Shotokan Karate dojos for several years and then became an officer on the Bloomington Police Force. He founded and became owner and Chief Instructor of the Mackinaw Valley Karate dojo and as a retired police officer, he is Director of Safety and Security in Bloomington High School, District 87. He is currently founder and Chairman of the Independent Traditional Karate Organization, ITKO.

FUNAKOSHI, Gichin: Considered to be the "Father of Modern Shotokan Karate-do." In Okinawa Funakoshi trained at karate daily from childhood to adulthood, while being a schoolteacher for 30 years. He formally introduced karate to mainland Japan. Critically helpful to karate's perpetual growth, Funakoshi created organized methods of teaching and refining karate-do, utilizing high-spirited intensive kata, basic technique, and self-defense training. He wisely utilized university clubs to establish respectable credibility for karate as he introduced his karate concepts to Japan. After WWII, Funakoshi and his students, including Nakayama and Nishiyama, founded the Japan Karate Association (JKA) and began the introduction of Shotokan karate to the world.

FLOWERS, Elston: Elston Flowers is a 6th Dan and member of the Central States Shotokan Shihankai. He is a Central Illinois Shotokan, senior instructor and has been featured in a recent em3Video DVD teaching. He has taught the Illinois Wesleyan University, karate accredited classes, IWU karate club programs, and coached the IWU karate team for decades. He is a co-director and instructor in the Central Illinois Shotokan Karate Association in Bloomington Illinois and teaches and directs classes at the Four-Seasons Karate, Central Illinois Shotokan Karate Association classes. Flowers is a retired professional High School Educator and school administrator.

FRAGUAS, Jose M.: Jose M. Fraguas was born in Madrid, Spain and started his martial arts training in judo when he was 9 years old and studied Shito-ryu karate under Japanese Master Masahiro Okada. He still follows his karate-do path with guidance from Okada Sensei. Jose Fraguas Sensei has trained, taught, written about, educated, and enlightened people about karate-do for well over four decades. He was a National Champion in both Kata and Kumite and was a member of the Organizational Committee of the 5th W.U.K.O. (WKF) World Championships. He is a prolific world-famous writer, editor, and publisher of hundreds of articles, more than 27 books on karate and martial arts, and many screenplays. As early as the age of 16, he started writing and contributing for publications across the United Kingdom, France, Germany, Spain, Italy, Portugal, Australia, Holland and the United States. In addition, he is a motivational speaker and a "Sports, Strength and Conditioning Specialist." He is the editor and publisher of Empire Books and *Masters Magazine*. Fraguas is an internationally recognized martial arts authority by karate masters around the world. He is a skilled fifth-degree black belt Shito-ryu karateka who in the early morning, trains daily, in addition to promoting quality martial arts through the publication realm. Jose currently lives in Los Angeles, California. He clearly reflects his philosophy that "writing is a reflection that you develop through training, and karate-do is a mindset and a tool to improve people's lives..."

GARLS, John: John Garls is an ASKA and Central States Shotokan 3rd Dan with over twenty years of training who is an assistant instructor in Pekin and Mapleton Dojos, and who retired from being a Technical Computer Supervisor at Caterpillar Tractor Company. Garls combines his tech skills with photography and karate skills to archive Central Illinois Shotokan Karate Association events. His latest video project was filming for the Central States, Spring 2019 Clinic DVD that was published by *em3Video* and sold on Amazon and in *Masters Magazine*. For years his DVDs have featured Midwest instructor classes and even national venues that highlight excellent Shotokan instruction.

HARTMAN, James: James Hartman is a 6th Dan in the Central States Shotokan and was promoted to 5th Dan in both the ASKA and WUKO with over four decades of training. Hartman is a senior Shihankai member in the Central States Shotokan, Technical Chairman and Program Director, and Senior Instructor in the Central Illinois Shotokan Karate Association in Pekin-Peoria area. He is a retired Peoria Police Officer who in addition to his normal duties, was a certified police Self-Defense Tactics and Firearm Tactics Instructor for over twenty-five years. Having started karate in the Pekin High School Karate Club in the 1970s., Hartman is a Shotokan Karate training veteran, seasoned competitor at local, state, and national and international levels. He has been published in *Shotokan Karate Magazine (SKM)*, and has written a book, *Beginner's Mind: A Boy's Journey to Manhood*. Hartman has also developed a "Fight Back" Self-Defense Program for women, as well as teaching regular karate classes for all levels. He taught numerous ASKA, Black Belt Development clinics, hosted by Sensei Randall G. Hassell. Hartman currently teaches Central States Shotokan Instructor Clinics and was recently featured in a Central States Shotokan Seminars DVD produced by em3Video.

HARTTER, Carl: Carl Hartter has over 45 years of Shotokan Karate training, competition, teaching experience. Hartter successfully ran business operations and programs at many Central Illinois locations. He was director and Chief Instructor of the Central Illinois Karate Association dojos and Central Illinois Shotokan dojos for decades. Carl Hartter is a 7th Dan, Chief Instructor and Director Emeritus of the Central Illinois Shotokan Karate Association, in Bloomington, IL, co-founder of the Central States Shotokan, and originally served on the founding Board of Directors and Shihankai of the American Shotokan Alliance (ASKA). He and his wife Elayne, a 6th Dan, have directed accredited karate classes at Illinois Wesleyan University; that was one of first few accredited college karate programs in the U.S. and it is still active. They currently live in Montana and Florida. Carl teaches clinics for the Central States Shotokan and other dojos by invitation.

HARTTER, Elayne: Elayne Hartter is a 6th Dan who began training in 1977 at Illinois Wesleyan University. On the Central States Shotokan Shihankai, Elayne has a rich karate history in training, competition, and teaching in university and commercial dojos. She has taught all ages in classes and clinics, and has successfully written curriculum, directed, and taught children's karate programs in the Central Illinois Karate Association and Central Illinois Shotokan.

HASSELL, Randall G.: Randall Hassell started training with Hidetaka Nishiyama when he was twelve years old. Hassell was the Chief Instructor and Founder of the American Shotokan

Karate Alliance (ASKA), and an original Co-Founder and President of the American JKA Karate Association (AJKA). He proudly developed and conducted the ASKA Black Belt Development Program and instructed clinics, seminars, and classes for all ages, literally travelling from coast to coast. His enthusiasm and knowledge of karate were amazing as he taught riveting classes, and especially his instructor clinics. He was the author, editor, and publisher of thirty books including: *Conversations with the Master: Masatoshi Nakayama, Shotokan Karate: Its History and Evolution, A Samurai Journey: Osamu Ozawa,* co-author (with Edmond Otis) of the *Complete Idiots Guide to Karate, Karate: Zen-Pen-Sword,* just to name a few! Randall Hassell Sensei wrote literally over a hundred articles on Karate-do published worldwide. He directed both Focus Publications and Tamashi Press publishing companies, publishing books and DVDs. He was certainly "Shotokan's Great Communicator!"

HEMP, Renee: Renee Hemp has been training for fifteen years and is a unique black belt instructor. She is the Director and Instructor for the Boys and Girls Club of Pekin continuing the program that has been continuously going for over 30 years. As a hobby, Sensei Renee runs marathons regularly. She is working on a doctorate in medicine as she trains and teaches. Renee is an excellent instructor and mentor for all karateka who she trains with.

HEMP, Pamela: Pam Hemp Sensei is a Nidan who has been training for nearly two decades and teaches regularly in

Central States Shotokan and Central Illinois Shotokan Karate Association dojos. As a retired nurse, her medical expertise is an asset in training programs. She is an excellent instructor for adults and youth alike and wonderful mentor for karateka of all ages.

HIROKAZU, Kanazawa: Hirokazu Kanazawa was a student of Master Gichin Funakoshi and a graduate of Takushoku University. He was one of original famous JKA international champion competitors and a premier instructor of the Japan Karate Association. Kanazawa then became founder and President of the Shotokan Karate International (SKI), with dojos in over 60 countries world-wide.

INGBER, Lester PhD: As a Shotokan karate sensei, and a PhD in Physics, Lester Ingber wrote the book, *Karate Kinematics and Dynamics*, in 1981. He was the president of the Physical Studies Institute (PSI) in California. In 1968, Ingber wrote a thesis on the physical and mental principles involved in karate techniques. Dr. Ingber presented his thesis to the Japan Karate Association (JKA) and the All-American Karate Federation (AAKF) and became the first Westerner to receive their instructor's degree. His thesis was published as *The Karate Instructor's Handbook* in 1976.

JENNINGS, Greg: Greg Jennings Sensei is a 3rd Dan in Shotokan who started training in 1981 in the Pekin HS Karate club and competed both regionally and nationally for many years. He also trained for many years in Wushu. He had the opportunity to train in China with the Wushu Beijing Team led by Wu Bin, who happened to have bee Jet Li's instructor. Jennings trains primarily in Shotokan, and on his own often works at combining the relaxation of Wushu movement with his Shotokan kumite especially for self-defense.

JUREWICZ, Dennis: Dennis Jurewicz Sensei is a Nidan in the Central States Shotokan and has been training since his early days in the Pekin High School Karate club, and now as black belt, and assistant instructor in the Central Illinois Shotokan Karate Association for decades in all their dojos. He has a degree in computer security, is a federally trained computer intelligence security professional, and as a hobby, a firearms expert.

KAWAMOTO, Norio: Norio Kawamoto Sensei was a graduate of Takushoku University and a Commander of a Communications Squadron on Fuchu Airbase near Tokyo. One of his instructors was a monk in Mie Prefecture where Kawamoto took students to train in gasshuku. He was a senior Japan Self-Defense Force Team, JKA instructor, in the Hoitsugan. Kawamoto and Enoeda Sensei were warm friends and enjoyed seeing each other at Nippon Budokan Championships. Kawamoto Sensei like to say that, "A true karate instructor will never make money teaching karate." (Refer to Chapter 13.) He was Quinn Sensei's main instructor at the Hoitsugan for the military team and they became good friends.

KAWAWADA, Minoru: This is Kawawada Sensei's motto: "Strive NOT to be a master, but to BE a GOOD TEACHER."

One of Masatoshi Nakayama's most notable students is Minoru Kawawada. Kawawada Sensei, 8th Dan (now retired from the JKA but currently teaching at the Hoitsugan) started his karate training by taking tickets at the door for tournaments when he was 14 years old. Since then, karate has been his life. His mission. He grew to become a world-class competitor and instructor. In fact, under Nakayama's years of personal tutelage, and after Nakayama's passing, Kawawada become the Chief Instructor of the famed Hoitsugan dojo. In Master Nakayama's own home dojo, where international students for decades have come to live and train, Kawawada carries on the tradition to pass on his teacher's karate-do.

Minoru Kawawada, known as an astounding world class competitor, including one notable win as Grand Champion of the first World Shoto Cup Tournament with first place in both kata and kumite, is one of the superior Shotokan karate instructors of our day. For decades, my students and I have watched video in awe as he fought and performed kata in international competition. The pictures of him doing kata Sochin are clearly imprinted in our minds. He currently supervises and teaches at the Hoitsugan in Japan and travels on many continents worldwide to reach out and to teach karate-do. His instruction, advice, and historical perspectives on traditional karate are invaluable. Kawawada Sensei is one of the world's finest karate instructors.

KIM, Sonny: Sensei Sonny Kim was both a highly revered karate instructor and a highly decorated police officer in the Cincinnati Police Department and was sadly shot and killed in the line of duty. Kim Sensei was born in South Korea, attended Truman High School in Chicago and the University of Cincinnati and was a police officer for 27 years. He was highly respected in Shotokan and all karate circles, and his students and instructors still carry on karate in his honor and legacy.

KEELING, Jon: Jon Keeling is the Chief Instructor of Silicon Valley Karate, formerly JKA of Silicon Valley, and has been teaching since he founded Silicon Valley Karate in 1998. He is a graduate of the University of California, Berkeley and began a career in finance in 1991 for superior firms and help Japanese clients on the West Coast. Keeling Sensei lived at the Hoitsugan from 1985 to 1988, the summer 1990 and for a few other short stays. He lived & trained in Tokyo for a total of 8 years and for a few years taught many Saturday classes at the Hoitsugan, on Hoitsugan kata teams that placed 3rd, 2nd and 1st in different years at the JKA All-Tokyo Championships. Jon has been the author of over 100 Karate-related articles and started teaching Karate in 1984. He is respected worldwide as a leader in Shotokan Karate, and hosts many internationally renowned clinics featuring Hoitsugan instructors, including Minoru Kawawada, Chief Instructor of the Hoitsugan dojo, from Ebisu, Japan.

KERRN, Tim: Tim Kerrn Sensei started karate in the early 2006. Kerrn is a 3rd Dan who has been competing, as well as assisting with, and teaching in all Central Illinois Shotokan Karate, YWCA karate classes, park district rec-center programs, and other dojos as well as. He is a law enforcement officer and served in the Peoria Park District Police and works as a security officer and an armed guard for a private firm.

LAWRENCE, Trenton: Lawrence Sensei is a humble karateka and black belt who is always willing to help mentor and teach whenever possible. He started karate at age seven in the Pekin Boys and Girls club program and continues training today. He has run a private tech-security business, been an NRA firearms instructor and is now full-time professional Agri-business person. He has often been helpful maintaining karate social media platforms for Central States Shotokan projects as well. He is, like many, many adult black belts, a devoted family member.

LUDOLPH, Cathy: Cathy Ludolph Sensei is the director of the Peoria Area FFA and has started, managed, and taught the Peoria County area Central Illinois Shotokan Karate club. She has also been an integral promoter and sensei in the Pekin and Mapleton area karate club classes.

McCABE, Michael: Michael McCabe started in the original Pekin High School Karate Club decades ago and has been training and teaching since. He is a Supervisor at Obrien Steel and although he travels nationwide, he always makes time to mentor and teach karate classes. Mike regular teaches classes in the Central Illinois Shotokan Karate classes and is a CSS and

ASKA 4th Dan. He has always been a strong karateka and teaches classes in Pekin and Mapleton dojos regularly, including the CISKA Saturday Morning Breakfast Club.

MICKLE, Jon-Paul: Jon-Paul Mickle Sensei started training in karate in 1986 in the Central Illinois Shotokan karate Association and became a certified black belt in the AJKA and the JKA as well. He merged his training with 27 years in the Air Force as a Colonel; Security Forces Commander. Mickle Sensei was a Professor, Air University, Texas Tech and the University of Washington. He credits karate for making it all possible for the magnitude in which he served his country.

Not long ago, he unexpectedly dropped into the author's dojo (could have knocked me over with a feather,) and told the class how karate had empowered his life to make the accomplishments he had made.

MIJAILOVIC, Val: Val Mijailovic Hanshi is CEO and Publisher of *Masters Magazine* and em3Video, from Sun Valley, California. He is a prolific film maker, producer, publisher, and a highly renowned 8th Dan karate instructor who has studied with Master Takayuki Kubota since 1970. Mijailovic is a three-decade veteran of national and international competition. He was the Winner of the 1st IKA World Championships. And was a member of the U.S. team competing in the Individual and Team Kumite at the 1977 World WUKO Cup in Japan. He won numerous championships throughout the 70s, 80s and 90s. He still trains and teaches under Soke Takayuki Kubota, Gosok Ryu Karate, International Karate Association. Val has also worked in the filming and documentary movie production and television industry, and he has showcased and championed Native American issues in his excellent work, as well. His latest work is a 5-DVD set called *Hard Core Karate,* that stresses an old school battlefield mind set for karate and competition techniques.

MUSASHI, Miyamoto: Musashi (1584-1634) is often referred to as "Kensei" or "Sword Saint" because he reportedly won 60 legendary duels to the death by the time he was in his early thirties. He was for the most part, a master-less samurai who wandered about testing his skills against various kendo masters. Often unknown, Musashi was also a superior artist, painter and wood carving sculptor, as well as swordsman. In his remaining years, Musashi retired to a cave to write his views and lessons on strategy in the form of his book, *Go Rin No Sho (Book of Five Rings).* This book, among other things, is unique because it is written in the first person, with Musashi teaching the reader his thoughts on strategy for individual combat and war.

Go Rin No Sho is every bit as valuable today as it is often useful and popular for strategies in business centers in Japan, and on Wall Street, just as it is in martial arts dojos and war. This author found Musashi's book, *Go Rin No Sho,* on Michigan Avenue, on Chicago, Illinois' "Gold Coast," in the business section of a bookstore, still providing the "competitive edge."

NAKAYAMA, Masatoshi: Master Nakayama (1913-1987) was a direct student of Gichin Funakoshi and after WWII became the

Chief Instructor of the Japan Karate Association (JKA). He assisted Funakoshi in helping create the technical standards and curriculum so that the JKA was officially recognized by the Ministry of Education of Japan. Nakayama wrote many of the first and most authoritative texts on karate, samples include the *Best Karate* eleven volume set, and the famous and standard setting *Dynamic Karate*. Two other excellent resources for additional information about Nakayama are, *Conversations with the Master: Masatoshi Nakayama*, by Randall Hassell, and *Karate Masters, Vol. 1*, by Jose Fraguas.

NISHIYAMA, Hidetaka: Hidetaka Nishiyama was a direct student of Gichin Funakoshi starting in the early 1940s, and he is not at all hard to find even if you are viewing historic karate videos of the Funakoshi era. He was one of the leaders of the JKA and wrote *Karate: The Art of Empty-Hand Fighting*. In 1961, Nishiyama moved to the United States where he formed the America Amateur Karate Federation (AAKF) and later founded the International Traditional Karate Federation (ITKF).

OEDEWALDT, Kevin: Kevin Oedewaldt is a 4th Dan in the Central States Shotokan and ASKA, who has been studying and teaching Shotokan for over 25 years. He graduated from Western Illinois University, where he trained with Sensei Ed Kuras, and has been in the Central Illinois Shotokan Karate Association for decades. Kevin has been a youth program club director and instructor and has a special talent for teaching youth. Kevin and family live and teach in Peoria County, in Illinois.

OTIS, Edmond: Edmond Otis is an internationally known instructor, competitor, coach, and judge. He is one of a handful of the most unique and extremely popular, inspiring, and motivating American instructors. His classes, like his *Essential Shotokan* video sets are rich with technical information. Otis also co-authored *The Complete Idiot's Guide to Karate* with Randall Hassell. Otis is a licensed psychotherapist who presents and coaches groups, businesses, and organizations, on using martial arts principals to meet their corporate and individual needs. Edmond Otis was the Shihankai Chairman of the American Shotokan Karate Alliance (ASKA), and the chairman of the American JKA Karate Association (AJKA). Otis is an internationally famous instructor and motivational speaker.

OZAWA, Osamu: Osamu Ozawa was the most senior Japanese karate master in the Western Hemisphere when he died in 1998. He was born in Kobe, Japan, and first trained in Wado-ryu. He often told us a wonderfully charming story about "starting karate because" he "was so terrible in baseball!" At age 17, attending Hosei University, he trained directly under Gichin Funakoshi.

He passionately wanted to be a warrior and joined the Japanese Imperial Navy as a pilot. Crashing on takeoff and receiving critical injuries ended his war abruptly. Weeks later, arriving home, he found a flat barren landscape from a nuclear blast. Lying in the dirt was a splintered board with some barely readable directions to the survivors of the Ozawa family.

When Ozawa found his family, they were shocked to see him. (He told us their eyes were very big!) They thought he was lost in the war and had held his funeral weeks before. Ozawa's amazing life showcased his incredibly positive attitude and belief in the real power of karate-do. He rose from ashes to be a millionaire and pauper many times. You can read it in his own words in the book, *A Samurai Journey: Osamu Ozawa*, by Randall Hassell.

QUINN, Ted: Ted Quinn is a 6th dan, Senior Instructor, and Technical Adviser in the Central Illinois Shotokan Karate Association, and on the Shihankai of the Central States Shotokan. Quinn started karate training in 1975, in the Pekin High School karate club with Rick Brewer Sensei in the Central Illinois Shotokan Karate Association. After joining the Air Force working with Intelligence Processing, and was stationed in Japan, living with his family for over 12 years, training, competing, and teaching in Japan Karate Association (JKA) classes. For his first six years in Japan, he trained at the Hoitsugan dojo in Ebisu, Tokyo, and competed in the Budokan, a member of the Japanese Defense Force Karate Team. He also won 2nd Place in kata in the All-Japan Self-Defense Force Championships and was presented the trophy by the Japanese Minister of Defense. He received recognition for being an "Ambassador of Friendship" between countries from the USAF. His last 6 years in the air force were spent stationed at the Misawa Air Force base, where he also taught JKA classes and competed in the Nippon Budokan on the Misawa team. He reads, writes, and speaks fluently in Japanese. Quinn currently teaches in the Central Illinois Shotokan Karate Association.

SCHMIDT, Stan: Stan Schmidt earned the rank of 8th Dan from the Japan Karate Association (JKA) and was the first non-Japanese to be awarded the title of *Shihan* from the Japan Karate Association. Three of Schmidt's books, *Spirit of the Empty Hand, Recognition,* and *Meeting Myself: Beyond Spirit of the Empty Hand,* are clearly as inspiring as his clinics.

When he came to teach ASKA clinics in St. Charles, MO, and in Central Illinois, he often told a story about using a stone for a "makiwara" as he lay in bed in the hospital with a double hip replacement. He said that in the first karate book he ever read, it said, "The karate man must train every day." And that as he lay in pain, he remembered that book, so to distract himself from thinking about the pain, he would punch a rock. How can you not be inspired about such a karate instructor? His books and DVDs, with his stories of training with instructors like Nakayama, Enoeda, Tanaka, Sugiura, Kase, and the like, speak volumes.

SOHO, Takuan: Takuan Soho lived between 1573-1645, and was a proponent of the *Rin-zai* Sect of *Zen*. He was famous for his clever, rather dry, wit and his admirably strong character. He has been reportedly a strong influence on Miyamoto Musashi in most of the literature and the Japanese movies about Musashi's life, trials and tribulations. Takuan, was known to be an abundant writer, gardener, poet, tea master, and artist and calligrapher. According to the literature and legend, he was both a friend and teacher to Musashi, who was a swordsman, artist, and *ronin* ("wave man" or "masterless samurai"). But according to literature and legend, Takuan was also a teacher to the Emperor and the Shogun. According to his own book, *The Unfettered Mind* (translated by William Scott Wilson), Takuan was able to move freely from student to student, high or low classes, with ease; and he never became narcissistic over his fame.

SPENNY, Tammy: Tammy Spenny Sensei trained and taught karate for many years in the Central States Shotokan, Mapleton dojos. Coming up through the ranks, she and her daughters trained in the ASKA together, and as a black belt, she was an exceptional sensei and mentor for all ages and especially young people. She represents the best in karate. Her unexpected passing this year was a great loss to the Central States Shotokan.

STAHLY, Jim: Jim Stahly started training in 1989 and has trained, competed and taught karate continuously for 30 years. He is the co-director of the Central Illinois Shotokan Karate Association in Bloomington, Illinois. Jim is a professional in advertising for State Farm Insurance and has written and had many karate articles published in Shotokan Karate Magazine and other publications. Stahly teaches all ages in classes and clinics at the Four-Seasons Club in Bloomington. He is a 5th Dan in the Central States Shotokan (and ASKA) who regularly teaches CSS Instructor and Black Belt Development Clinics.

SUGIYAMA, Shojiro: Shojiro Sugiyama was born in Tokyo (Yotsuya), Japan in 1929. Before joining the Japan Karate Association in 1954, he had trained in two other karate styles. He came to the USA, to Chicago, Illinois, to teach for the JKA in 1963. Literally thousands of students, both beginner and advanced, since that time, have been introduced or enlightened by the training in Sugiyama Sensei's Midwest dojos. Whether taught by Sugiyama himself, or by the many honored guest instructors like Hidetaka Nishiyama, there are thousands of black belts and their students world-wide who are affected by his work. His books, *Karate, Synchronization of Body and Mind* and *25 Shotokan Kata* (in English, Spanish, and Japanese) are a training fixture in countless gym bags and dojo bookshelves. With the students, books, classes, and the lessons learned by all, you can easily see the contributions of Shojiro Sugiyama and his Great Lakes brand of JKA Karate.

TANAKA, Masahiko: According to an article by Stan Schmidt, Tanaka originally went to Nihon University to study veterinarian medicine and forestry, and even envisioned owning a farm in South America. At the age of 20 a friend invited Tanaka to visit a karate class taught by Yaguchi Sensei. He was hooked! After college he was a Sandan and he wanted to become a student instructor at the Japan Karate Association. They refused him because of lack of funding to pay for student instructors, but they told him if he could support himself, he could stay and train in the "Hornets' Nest".

He worked odd jobs from being a river man, literally balancing on moving logs in the water, to selling real estate.

He often credited his strong stances and powerful movements to being on the logs. As an example of mental tenacity, Tanaka entered the All-Japan JKA National Championships 12 times before winning. Then in 1975 went on to win the world title in Los Angeles California. Of crucial importance to the theme of this book, and to all those reading it, in an interview with Jose Fraguas, Tanaka says, "Karate training is a mirror of life, and the way you live your life must go hand in hand with the way you train."

TOMM, Geoff: Geoff Tomm Sensei started training in the early 1990s at the Central Illinois Shotokan when he was seven years old. He has continued since then incorporating karate-do into his life, even while serving his country including two tours in Afghanistan. During that time, he was promoted to Shodan training with Sensei Cathy Cline and was promoted to Nidan by Okazaki Shihan. Tomm trains and teaches in Anchorage Alaska, where he attends in the University of Alaska finishing up his Masters' degree in Science and Project Management.

TRAVERS, Chris: Chris Travers started training in 1974 at Illinois State University, and is a 6th Dan, and Shihankai member of the Central States Shotokan. He was recently featured teaching an Instructor Training Clinic in an em3Video, Central States Shotokan Spring Clinic, DVD in 2019. Chris is the Chief Instructor and Director of the Elmhurst Shotokan Karate Club, Elmhurst Illinois.

TURNER, Geoff: Geoff Turner has been an inspiration in the Central States Shotokan and Midwest dojos for many years. He was an aspirational leader in the Pekin, Illinois area, and in the ASKA clinics when he moved to St. Louis area. From early in his training, he began to have breathing issues until he literally needed oxygen in class. But he kept training, determined, lean and tough. Senior black belts remember him literally going across the floor to use his inhalers, then to turn and repeat. Geoff Turner, as a leader in karate was active in his community and a friend of everyone and willing to mentor and help. Over ten years ago he had a double lung transplant and was visiting with a group of fellow black belt friends the very day he came out of surgery. Since then, he remained as active as possible with karate, shooting, and all his friends. Sadly, he passed away in 2020 with complications of the coronavirus. But still, he inspired all who knew him, proudly fighting with his karate spirit.

TZU, Sun: Sun Tzu is probably most noted in modern times from *The Art of War*. Among the many Chinese classics read by Funakoshi and his peers that the work of Sun Tzu was included and was of great value. Clearly the Japanese military studied his work. Written more than 2000 years ago, around 500 B.C., the essays and works of Sun Tzu may have been the first time the intensive study of combat and war were verbalized and written down for future generations. Even Napoleon was purported to have studied Sun Tzu's work. One very interesting parallel for traditional martial artists and Budo, is that Sun Tzu stressed that just having the power and strength were not enough to win. He taught that intellect, morals and the quality of the use of strategic resources and methods were more important than raw might.

WOOD, Gary: Sensei Gary Wood was a Shodan who was instrumental in mentoring youth and assisting as an instructor in the Pekin Dojos for many years. He was a school counselor at Pekin Community High School and helped run and sponsor the PCHS Karate Club to cause it to be the highly unique success that it was and resulted in the club lasting well over 30 years. In the late 1970s, he was also responsible for encouraging and guiding the author, in writing the textbook, curriculum, and structuring the Accredited Karate Class; as they educated the students, faculty, administration, School Board Members, and the like, to have perhaps the first fully accredited (credits counting toward a High School diploma) public high school Karate Class in the US. Many of the students he mentored have become exemplary citizens and senior karate instructors that still teach. He lived a life of humility and service to others: the karate way.

YABE, James: Even now, James Yabe's technique is jaw-dropping. He lived and trained in Japan training with Nakayama Sensei in Japan in the 1960s, having been involved in karate since the 1950s. In 1961, he was the first All-America Karate Tournament Champion in both Kumite and Kata. He continued to dominate the American Shotokan scene by winning again in 1962, 1963, 1966, and again in 1967. He was a member of U.S. National Team at the 1970 WUKO

Championships in Japan and the 1972 WUKO Championship in Paris. Since he began training in 1958, Yabe has trained with some of the most renowned karate masters in the United States and in Japan, and he is one of the most senior students of Hidetaka Nishiyama in the U.S. His technique is mesmerizing, his teaching abilities are exemplary. He spontaneously conveys his genuine passion and love for karate-do in every movement.

Glossary of Terms

Basai Dai: "Basai Dai" means "To Penetrate a Fortress" and is an advanced kata that is also studied in different styles and in other forms under other names such as *Patsai or Passai*. In Shotokan karate both *Basai Dai* and *Basai Sho* are taught. Basai Dai is characterized by strong techniques and hip rotations and it can be traced back to Master Itosu, one of Gichin Funakoshi's instructors.

Budo: In simplest form, *"Bu"* can mean "warrior" and *"do"* means "the way." "Bu" can also mean reconciliation, harmony, or to stop fighting. So additionally, Budo can mean, "The way of being a peaceful warrior."

Bunkai: The meaning or application of the techniques in kata, and an excellent way to teach kata in a manner that is meaningful and more easily remembered is to study how the techniques are used.

Dan: A level of black belt.

Dojo: A school, room, or place that karate and other martial arts are studied. "Do" means the "way" and "jo" means the "place." Therefore, a dojo is the place where the "way" is studied.

Dojo Kun: Proper principles of attitude and conduct for all of those who train in a dojo Funakoshi condensed many "ideals" into five, generally known as the "Dojo Kun" that are often posted in a dojo for students to read and practice. Sometimes they are announced at the beginning or end of karate classes in a formal ceremony.

Gi: A common term used for karate uniform.

Godan: Fifth degree or fifth level of black belt, or in *Heian Godan* for example, it means the fifth level of the Heian kata "*Go*" means fifth and "*dan*" means level.

Go No Sen: Seizing the initiative later. Generally speaking, it means to let the opponent attack, and the block and counter, seizing the initiative, after your opponent's tactics are exposed.

Hajime: To begin, as in the command "Hajime!"

Heian: "Heian" is the name given to the most often used, first five basic kata in Shotokan karate training. Heian means "peaceful." Kata "Heian Shodan" would mean "Peaceful kata-level one." Likewise, kata "Heian Godan" would mean "Peaceful kata number five," or level five. In other styles of karate-do they are called "Pinan."

Ichi: One.

Ippon: One full point.

Japan Self-Defense Force: Japanese military forces.

Kami: Divinity or godlike.

Kamikaze: "*Kame*" means "divine," and "*kaze*" means "wind." Therefore, *kamikaze* literally means "divine wind." *Kamikaze* was the name given to Japanese suicide pilots used and noted especially toward the end of World War II.

Kanji: Japanese writing/calligraphy.

Karate: "*Kara*" means "empty," and "*te*" means "hand." Therefore, "*karate*" means "empty hand." *Karate* is an unarmed Japanese martial art using parts of the body as weapons. There are many styles and organizations teaching quality traditional karate world-wide. Typically, the whole body is used, combining the mind and the body, to perform punches, kicks, blocks, sweeps and throwing in a combined manner to defeat the opponent. At the same time in traditional styles of karate, students are required to build positive character traits, and demonstrate good citizenship.

Karate-do: "Karate" is "empty hand," and "do" means "way." *Karate-do* implies that one trains at karate for much more than sport, recreational hobby, or for mere exercise and entertainment. *Karate-do* means it is more of a combined physical and mental lifestyle that improves the way one might conduct him or herself.

Karateka: A karate student

Katana: The long sword with a convex, one-edged blade, carried by *Samurai*. It was worn with its cutting edge up so that it could be quickly drawn and swiftly used.

Kata: Prearranged formal exercises, comprised of multiple techniques that allow the participant to improved karate skills without the need of a training partner. Kata allow students to practice techniques in combinations, and from different angles, as if to defend themselves from multiple attackers from different directions and scenarios.

Kensei: Teacher of the art of the sword.

Kiai: A high-spirited shout that accompanies karate techniques. Sometimes called a "spirit-shout," it is meant to startle the opponent and at the same time give the karate practitioner an extra shot of adrenalin, energy, and confidence. Physiologically a *"kiai"* is a sharp, short, very loud outburst of noise, combined with breathing exhalation that helps you use muscle groups more efficiently for more strength and power. Mentally it helps you to focus your energy into the task at hand.

Kihon: Basic karate technique.

Kohai: "Kohai" refers to another student who is "junior" to you in rank in the dojo.

Kumite: Sparring

Kuzushi: To destabilize or crush the opponent's balance and posture.

Maii: Distance.

Makiwara: Traditional punching board or punching post used in karate training to practice timing, breathing, relaxation, and tension all at the same time. Frequent and correct use of the makiwara has been historically used to toughen striking points on hands, feet, and the like. The physical and audio feed-back helps you understand and obtain the correct feeling of a focused technique.

Mizu No Kokoro: "Mind like water" is the general translation. A very calm and still pond accurately reflects all that is around it with crystal clarity, like a mirror. Likewise, a calm uncluttered mind can more clearly perceive all information, even the slightest bit of disruption or movement that the five senses can take in. Much like if the same pond is blasted with wind and rain, if the mind is cluttered with thoughts of fear and doubt, it cannot efficiently process perceptions and information accurately and swiftly. In the event of life-threatening circumstances, mistakes and incorrect reactions can mean life or death. Therefore, we train to remain calm in the face of challenging situations in the dojo, to improve the odds that we can do the same in real self-defense situations.

Mu: Empty; clear of anything; none. Example: "*Mushin*" — "*mu*" means "no," "*shin*" means "mind." *Mushin* means "no mind," the equivalent of an unattached mind clear of cluttering thoughts.

Musashi: Full name, *Shinmen Musashi No Kami Fugiwara No Genshin*, but he was most commonly called *Miyamoto Musashi*. Miyamoto Musashi was born in the 1580s in Japan. He is best known as the "Sword Saint" of Japan. Being a *ronan* (masterless *Samurai*) for much of his life, he roamed for many years sharpening his skills by challenging many *kendo* schools. He is best known for winning over sixty duels before retiring to a cave in order to write his strategies and philosophy in *Go Rin No Sho*, or *"Book of Five Rings."* His strategies appear nearly all Japanese martial arts since then and are still popular and extremely relevant today.

Mushin: "No mind." It refers to putting one's mind in a state of emptiness to be able to react swiftly and accurately to any threat. The mind is theoretically uncluttered with disruptive thoughts that would slow down reaction times. This way a trained individual's actions can come from the subconscious mind due to karate skill sets that are, as Master Gichin Funakoshi often said, "internalized."

Myo: Enlightenment gained from doing karate as a regular part of your life, so much incorporated into your lifestyle that you don't have to think about it.

Ni: Two.

Nukite: Spear hand thrust.

"Oss!" or "Osu!": Greetings often used between two martial artists to show mutual respect. This response or greeting can be used to show respect before training with a partner, or to begin and end a training session. Generally speaking, "*Osu!*" means to "persevere" and "push forward." It is an important response for students to give to instructors that shows that the student understands and is going to try hard to give their best effort. "*Oss!*" is also given at the end of a class or session in "thanks" for gratitude for being given a lesson by the *sensei*.

Samurai: The word Samurai means "to serve." Samurai were the top ruling military social class in Japan for several hundred years. Samurai were tremendously loyal to one lord. Only samurai were allowed to carry two swords.

San: Three.

Sempai: means "senior" in the relationship of age or ranking in the "*sempai-kohai*" (senior/junior) systems in traditional martial arts schools. The senior-junior (*sempai/kohai*) system often utilizes ranks and colored belts to indicate the levels of achievement, proficiency of *karate* skill sets, and knowledge. Even in the karate black belt levels, for example, there are graduated levels of competencies and achievement. Anyone higher than your current level or senior to you is your *sempai*.

Sen No Sen: To sieze the initiative earlier.

Sensei: Teacher/instructor.

Shi: Four.

Shihan: Senior instructor that other instructors and black belts look up to for guidance, instruction, and an example to follow.

Shihankai: A "Board" or "organizational body" composed of "senior instructors" (*Shihans*).

Shin: "Mind" or "heart."

Shodan: "First degree" black belt, or "first level" as used in kata "*Heian Shodan.*"

Shotokan: The traditional Japanese "karate style" developed, taught, and promoted by Master Gichin Funakoshi and his students.

Tsuki No Kokoro: "Mind like the moon." "*Tsuki No Kokoro*" is getting your mind globally aware of everything from large down to the smallest detail. The moon shines down on everything equally; it misses nothing. This is how the mind should be in the presence of danger. It is a state of awareness that is wide and acute at the same time.

Tsunami: Tidal wave.

Yame: Stop.

Zen: Unattached mind set. Karate is often called "moving *Zen*," because of the flowing unattached mental states karateka strive to be in when training.

www.ingramcontent.com/pod-product-compliance
Lightning Source LLC
Chambersburg PA
CBHW071957110526
44592CB00012B/1116